Beginner's Guide to House Plants

Also by Violet Stevenson

GARDENING WITH GREEN FINGERS

Beginner's Guide to House Plants

VIOLET STEVENSON

Pelham Books

First published in Great Britain by
PELHAM BOOKS LTD
52 Bedford Square
London, W.C.1
1973

ISBN 0 7207 0640 8

Set and printed in Great Britain by
Tonbridge Printers Ltd, Peach Hall Works, Tonbridge, Kent
in Baskerville eleven on twelve point
and bound by James Burn at Esher, Surrey

Contents

	Introduction	9
1	A Potted Look at Plants	11
2	The Easiest of All	24
3	Some Relatives of the Fig	31
4	Some Unexpected Lilies	39
5	Palms and Other Romantics	48
6	Just Like The Ivy	54
7	Plectranthus and Puddle Pots	61
8	Tree Lovers or Philodendrons	68
9	Vines Without Grapes	74
10	Happy Wanderers	78
11	The Prickly Subject of Cacti	83
12	The Many Names of Crassula	92
13	Bulbs are Nature's Prepacks	99
14	Flowering Plants in General	110
15	Preventions and Cures	120
	Index	134

List of Illustrations

Between pages 60 and 61
1 Plunging a saintpaulia
2 *Aechmea rhodocyanea* – an easy house plant
3 *Ficus benjamina*
4 Air-layering a *Ficus decora*
5 Sansevieria in flower
6 Group of house plants in bowl
7 *Phoenix dactylifera* – a decorative 'parlour' palm
8 Hedera (ivy) varieties
9 An easy-to-grow trailer – *Plectranthus fruticosus*
10 Two species of philodendron
11 Monstera growing into a plank of wood
12 Rhoicissus can be trained
13 *Cissus antarctica* – ideal for a sunless room
14 Tradescantia – a most popular house plant
15 Rooting tradescantia cuttings
16 A gorgeous leaf-flowing cactus in bloom
17 Succulent agave, aloe and cactus share a bowl
18 An echeveria in bloom
19 *Aeonium tabulaeforme*—a neighbour of the crassula family
20 Growing narcissi and hyacinths without soil

PICTURE CREDITS

The photographs in this book are by Leslie Johns

Introduction

Indoor gardening has become an essential part of modern life. It is interesting to note that as our world becomes more crowded, as buildings rise higher and as cities spread, so more and more people grow potted plants in their homes, offices and other places of work. Indeed, with no green leaf or growing plant nearby, many a person feels bereft – even though he or she may not always be aware of what it is that is missing. No wonder that a gift of a growing plant is received with such pleasure by both sexes and the young and old alike, and that millions of indoor plants are sold at all times of the year, not only at Christmas.

A gift plant is often the reason why some people become indoor gardeners. Because they have been successful in rearing one they feel confident enough to collect others. If, on the other hand, a person has been unsuccessful, he or she may feel regret for a time and then decide to have another go, usually after looking for an easier plant. Each type of gardener looks to the expert for guidance.

Others begin indoor gardening because they recognise this basic urge to grow something, to feel involved with nature if only in a small way. And one finds that if such people have never before grown any kind of house plant, they too are sure to ask which plants they should choose, what would be best to begin with.

This book sets out to help all new indoor gardeners by introducing them to individual plants which have proved to be tolerant and adaptable, as well as decorative and interesting in my own home. It should be possible, having read it, to take up indoor gardening with confidence and to continue enjoying it, relatively troublefree, for the rest of one's life.

At the same time I hope that those who, like me, have been indoor gardening for many years, will find something new in this fascinating occupation.

1. A Potted Look at Plants

The most important thing for an indoor gardener to remember at all times is that plants are living things and should be treated as such. It is a sad fact that one often sees some plant innocently subjected to treatment which should be meted out only to inanimate objects. All kinds of plants are expected to grow sitting over a radiator, in a deep puddle or high on a wall in a hot, arid air stream. I once saw several, each beautifully gift-wrapped, with only the tips of the leaves appearing above the paper, standing in a draughty corner of a dark living room where they had remained for a week at Christmas time. I fear whoever received one of them would have a dying plant to begin with. Yet they were bought and parcelled with love!

I like to remind people that house plants are horticultural pets and although they may be more varied than the animal kind they make much the same demands upon us. There are some, like cats, which will soon settle down practically anywhere so long as they are kept as warm as we like it ourselves, are fed, watered and groomed and allowed a certain degree of independence. Yet there are others, like tropical lizards to give an example, which need rather more specialised conditions with higher temperatures and humidity. They also need clean, unpolluted air, the right amount of light for the type, an occasional bathe and outing, as well as normal supplies of food and drink.

Unlike pets though, few plants demand special foods. What does for one suits many another, and this normally comes conveniently packeted in the form of potting composts or soils which can be easily enriched when necessary. But although a plant, again like an animal, is at the mercy of its owner, it cannot accept or reject the kind or quantity of food and drink which is offered. Consequently thousands of house plants die of starvation as well as over-feeding, of drought as well as drowning, and from being poisoned by toxic fumes in the atmosphere.

It often puzzles the inexperienced gardener to be told that it is very difficult to give him or her precise directions for looking after an individual, unseen plant, to declare without question whether or not it will flourish in a particular living room, how often it will require to be watered, if it will need feeding or to estimate the mature dimensions of a young and newly received plant. It is just as difficult to diagnose the reasons for the death of a plant one has never seen in a house or district one has never visited. Everything depends upon the environment in which the plant is growing. Some rooms are warm and well windowed, others are not, some are draughty or stuffy and plants will behave differently according to the stimuli they receive. Yet fortunately there are many agreeable and adaptable plants about which we can fairly safely generalise, and as all of these are both plentiful and easily obtainable I propose to make them the theme of this book.

But before I introduce them there are a few other important things to be discussed, matters on which rest the probabilities of success or failure of indoor gardening, for it is not enough to set down a tolerably house-hardy plant and hope for the best.

We should realise that a plant growing in a container indoors is subjected to a disturbing variety of conditions that it would not meet growing naturally outdoors in its native soil. In the first place it is extremely confined, more tightly caged than a canary! While in many instances the shoots and leaves might be able to grow high, wide and handsome, the roots are squeezed into a very small space. In the open a plant's roots stretch for considerable and often surprisingly great distances from the actual plant as they roam in their quest for essential plant foods and for moisture in the soil. In a pot a plant has to grow its roots differently. There is no room to travel except in a circle around and around the wall of the pot. Sometimes if you knock out a plant from its pot and inspect the roots you can see one or more which has been formed into a spiral because it has travelled round and round inside the confines of its home. The roots have formed a root ball. When a plant has been growing in a container for a long period roots become so numerous that they eventually form a tight mass, leaving little room for soil or water. Consequently, if no corrective action is taken, the plant becomes starved, for it has previously consumed all the soil which normally holds both food and drink for the plant. We say that such a plant has become pot-bound and that it needs re-potting.

When we do this we transfer the plant, not as you might expect to a very large pot with plenty of space for the roots and a considerable amount of new soil for them to explore, but to a pot just one size larger than the old one. And it is also important that the new soil we place around the old, spent root ball is as near to the original density as we can make it. To achieve this we have to ram the new soil to compact it. If we do not do this then the old roots tend to stay in the original mass and fail to benefit from their move or the addition of the new, food-rich, soil.

Obviously it is best to keep an eye on plants, and re-pot them before they get into this state. As a rule we get an indication when we see a root or two beginning to grow through drainage holes at the base of the pot. It is also possible to uncover the root ball and examine it from time to time, and this one should do after a certain interval, which will vary with plants and types of plants.

It always fascinates me to see how easy it is to tell that a starved plant has been re-potted, because the leaves and growth it makes after its move are larger and generally more lush than those below them. Sometimes it is hard to imagine that they were produced by the same plant.

You can tell from this that the quality of the soil in which pot plants are grown is important. It is more than a mere anchorage for the roots. When a plant is potted by a good grower it is rooted in soil which contains all the essential plant foods as well as other ingredients which are necessary if the roots are to remain healthy and functional. Most potting soils and composts (in this case the term means a soil mixture) are the result of many months of experiment and trial. Where at one time one kind of plant would be grown only in its own, special, individual compost of soil and other materials such as leafmould, peat, rotted turves, animal manures, lime, sand, chalk, soot, crushed brick and chemicals of various kinds, and where growers often had their own, secret composts to which they attributed their success, now it is much more likely that one great mix is used for a considerable number and variety of plants.

There are certain recipes which were devised by scientists at the John Innes Horticultural Institution which are faithfully, and no doubt gratefully, followed by some growers and certainly by countless gardeners. These mixtures cater respectively for seed sowing, for young plants and for those which are mature or which will have to remain for some time in one container. One important factor in their making is that the soil or loam used is sterilised before it is blended with the other ingredients. It is therefore not only bacteria and insect-free, but is also without any viable weed seeds that might later germinate, to the annoyance and confusion of the gardener and at the expense of the proper resident of the pot.

The John Innes (or J.I. as they are usually called) composts have been followed by others marketed by the great chemical combines such as I.C.I., Fisons and Pan Britannica Industries. These later mixtures are no-soil composts, which means that peat is used as the base, and they are more uniform in texture and content. These commercial composts have been so improved that it is possible now to buy one type, Kerimure, marketed by I.C.I., which will do for seed sowing as well as for final potting, and for plants which like lime as well as for those which dislike it. The need or dislike of certain plants for lime is an important point which will be discussed later.

When we realise that the old, pre-J.I. composts were likely to produce weeds as well as the required pot plant and that they were also likely to contain insect pests and fungal diseases, we can clearly see how important and helpful was the introduction of the new, scientifically balanced and sterile mixtures. These guaranteed the grower who used them a uniform and healthy batch of plants. Equally important is the fact that both the J.I. and the new commercial composts are easily available to the amateur and are on sale everywhere, well packed and easy and pleasant to use. The no-soil composts have a further point in their favour: compared with those which are soil-based they are extremely light in weight, an important factor if your indoor garden is several floors about street level or if you have to carry the bag home from the store. One finds also that there are not so many problems due to incorrect watering when they are used, and this seems to be due to the fact that peat holds water differently from soil, but more of this later.

Quite often a new plant owner will write to me to say that the plant appears to be in a very small pot and asks if it should be re-potted right away. I usually reply that if there is no sign of roots coming through the holes at the base of the pot the plant should be left as it is. As a rule a plant fresh from a nursery is all right for about six months, but by the end of this time the supplies of plant foods in the soil will be getting exhausted, although this depends on the time of year and the consequent vigour with which the plant is growing.

This is not due entirely to the fact that the plant has been growing strongly at their expense. Because the soil in a pot has to be watered so often and because the plant foods are in solution in it, a certain proportion of them become washed away, wasted or leached out as the water courses through the soil.

Often, instead of re-potting (this is not always convenient nor practical, as we shall see) we can restore the fertility of the soil and so adjust the balance of foods present by recharging it with soluble foods. These are added to the water, either at intervals or in some cases regularly at certain times of the year. Some plants need more food than others. From the decorative point of view some put on a better performance when they are starving! Some need more food only at certain stages of their life cycle, just before they flower, for example, while others may require a regular feeding at all times. For instance I have a large, climbing rhoicissus which for many years now has grown in the same soil in the same container, which sometimes looks quite ridiculously small for the size of the plant. There can be little real soil left around the roots. The plant is now entirely dependent on its regular ration of liquid food for its continued health, and fortunately a rhoicissus such as this will lead such an existence quite happily. Not all plants are as tolerant.

The new gardener has to learn not to be too generous. To give too much food in one dose is as harmful as allowing the plant to starve to death, and results are usually dramatic and quick! However, more details on feeding will be imparted as we reach other sections of this book. The important thing to realise at this point is that potting composts must be both well balanced nutritiously and hygienically, and that it is cheaper in the long run either to buy or to prepare a good mixture than to dig up free soil from the ground.

Apart from the question of food and plant pests, there is also another reason why it is false economy to try to save on soil. It is is important that a potting compost should be of the correct texture. There are some types mixed specially for certain plants (that for orchids is an example) in which others might find it impossible to grow. But even for the easy plants we have under discussion the soil must be properly mixed.

A potting compost has to be retentive of water yet it must never be waterlogged nor sodden. It must have sufficient body incorporated in it to ensure that it retains useful amounts of moisture so that this is readily available to the plant's roots, yet it must also be what gardeners term 'open' enough to contain plenty of air spaces, for roots need fresh air just as much as the other parts of the plant which happen to be above soil level.

If properly mixed open compost is allowed to become too dry, too many air spaces will be present and these will threaten the well-being of the plant. Left, literally, in the air, the roots can find no moisture and so begin to shrivel. Sometimes the root ball shrinks away from the inside of the pot to which it has held fast while it contained sufficient moisture, thus perilously creating an air space all around it. Sometimes, no matter how much water is given later, such roots can never be restored and the plant will die. Azaleas and heathers are examples of plants which can suffer this way.

Dry roots cannot perform their functions and conduct water to the upper parts of the plant as they should do. This is why it is harmful to let a plant go too long without water, unless it has its own built-in reservoir, such as that possessed by cacti and succulents. A plant in this situation will soon show signs of distress. Its leaves will grow limp and soon the whole plant wilts or flags, usually downwards from the tip. Sometimes first aid in the form of a quick plunge in a bucket of water will restore the plant almost magically, but too often it is too far gone to be revived. This is a fate which often befalls plants at Christmas time when they may not have been properly watered before being sent out from a shop and then are left standing in a hot, dry atmosphere while everyone is too occupied to attend to them.

Fortunately, as one handles more and more plants it becomes increasingly easy to spot the thirsty ones at a glance. There are also simple and attractive ways of preventing rapid moisture loss.

Once the compost is watered the air is driven out and water fills the tiny crevices instead, and if the right materials are present this water is held captive until it is taken up by the roots. As the water is absorbed air gradually fills the spaces again.

Actually, in many cases as I shall explain later it is beneficial to allow the compost to become dry, almost, but never quite, to danger point, because then when the water is poured over the surface it courses quickly down through the compost dragging a rush of fresh air with it as it squeezes out the old. This cleanses and purifies the soil. So, when we grow a plant in a pot we have to ensure that the compost or soil can become well aerated from time to time.

If soil is dug up from the garden or countryside and immediately put to use in a pot it is more than likely that it will react in quite a different manner than that expected.

In its true environment it is aerated by natural processes and over a longer period, not only by fluctuating periods of rain and drought, but also by burrowing worms and other creatures. In gardens it is usually more intensively cultivated and consequently well aerated. And we must not forget that the plants which grow in it outdoors have quite a different root system from the confined pot plants. The far-reaching roots play an important part in aerating the very soil in which they roam.

So don't be tempted! Although the soil may appear to be supporting goods plants outdoors it does not follow that it will continue to do so once it is removed and placed in a container. Unless it is made open, mixed with peat, well rotted leafmould and coarse clean sand or grit, it is likely to become quickly waterlogged and then panned. I have seen such soil form a cement-like sand pie when turned out of its pot.

If a new indoor gardener grasps the fact that air and water are interchangeable and that a plant needs both, I think that an important factor has been recognised and that success is sure to follow.

The way to water plants is, and I fear sometimes remains, a mystery to many people. I have to stress, and possibly shall do so time and time again, that more plants are killed by drowning than by any other means. I hope that I have shown that it is important to build up an air supply in the soil before adding more water. Having said this I hope that it will be obvious that this cannot be done if a small amount of water is poured over the soil surface each day.

We are bond to come across exceptions, and these will be considered as they arise should this be necessary, but for the general range of house-hardy plants the soil must be given a chance to become almost dry before it is recharged with moisture. If roots have to remain in wet, unaerated soil, which incidentally is also often low in temperature, they will die, and so will the rest of the plant. Not being aquatic plants which obviously thrive in such conditions, they simply cannot function. A plant often tries to grow under adverse conditions but finally the leaves become yellow and sickly and the plant dies.

Where a plant grows isolated, standing perhaps in a saucer, it is a simple matter to lift it and test its weight. Obviously a pot of dry soil is lighter in weight than one containing a wet mass.

Plants newly introduced to a home often suffer, mainly, I think, because the owner is too anxious that they should not die of neglect. Unfortunately it is the reverse which is most often true and they are killed by kindness!

It is not really possible to over-water a plant which has become pot-bound, simply because there is not sufficient soil to hold the moisture. But it is a very different matter with a newly potted plant whose roots have not yet filled the container.

House plants have been drawn from all sections of the plant world and although we have domesticated them to a certain degree, they retain their characteristics. Thus we have some plants which originate in warm, steamy jungles and demand from us steady warmth, humidity and shade; others which are swamp or water-marginal which like to paddle and which will, in fact, grow in pebbles and water if we wish them to do so; other from the desert which need sunshine and a long period of drought before being freely watered, to mention only three types. This means that so far as watering is concerned we find that some house plants must be constantly tended whilst others, like cacti, can be left without water for a month or so at certain periods of the year or at certain points in their development.

The size and type of pot and the way it is displayed or hidden has a bearing on how often it needs to be watered. A thirsty plant growing in a small, exposed container will need more frequent attention than a desert plant in a large container placed inside another vessel. There are ways we can keep some thirsty plants supplied with moisture without being involved in too much work ourselves.

When I first became interested in gardening the clay or terracotta pot was in universal use and we recognised and identified the sizes by terms given to them according to the numbers which could be made from a cast of clay. Thus a "sixty" was a pot 3 inches in diameter at the top and $3\frac{1}{2}$ inches deep, whereas a 'two' was 18 inches across the top and 14 inches deep.

Now it is the plastic pot that we are most likely to find and these come in more shapes and sizes than the old clay types. Nurserymen, who after all grow millions of pot plants, have found that these meet their requirements quite well. Plants appear to grow as well in plastic as in clay. Plastic pots are considerably cheaper so far as transport is concerned, for they are very light to handle, as anyone who has had to unload a lorry full of flower pots will tell you.

There are some people who believe that there is none so good as the natural clay pot. This is porous and moisture can both escape and enter through the sides of the pot. Plastic pots are not porous, although like the clay pots they are provided with drainage holes in the base.

If you sink a planted clay pot inside another, larger one and pack some moist material such as peat or sand below and all around the pot and see that this is kept moist, the water outside will gradually percolate through and be available to the roots inside. This method of sinking one pot inside another is known as plunging.

Apart from the obvious advantages to the roots of a plant the moist plunge bed also provides essential humidity to the leaves and upper portion of the plant. This is such a simple and efficient way of providing humidity. It can also be decorative, for the outer containers which hold the plunge bed can be as attractive as you wish. Further, they can hold more than one plant. Large bowls, vases, tubs, troughs and only a few of the many types of containers in which house plants look well.

Although moisture will not penetrate through the walls of a plastic pot, any plant it holds when plunged inside another container will still benefit from the humidity released. And if a good layer of moist plunge material is provided below its base some moisture will enter the pot through the drainage holes. Further, if when the plunge medium is packed around the plant pot we ensure that it reaches just a little above rim level and that the merest layer is spread over the pot soil surface, the result is much the same as with a clay pot.

It is important that the plunge medium remains moist but not sodden. Often it is enough merely to keep this moist, but there are likely to be certain times of the year when growth is more active, or when the plant is flowering, when it will need to be watered through the soil in the pot in the usual way as well as through the plunge material.

Many an indoor gardener has complained to me that he or she just cannot grow certain plants, African violets in particular, yet once I can persuade them to change to the plunge method success follows. After all, a plant growing this way, though still captive is just a little nearer to a more natural style of growth than if its pot stood exposed on all sides to the hot, drying influences of the modern home.

A good modern plant nursery is as clean as science can make it. A commercial grower cannot afford to lose his stock through any kind of infestation, either of insects or fungal spores. Fortunately it is much easier to control pests within glass walls than it is in the great outdoors. A house full of tens of thousands of one kind of house plant all in gleaming good health is a fine and reassuring sight.

Furthermore, most plants are given a final prophylactic spray or polish before they leave the nursery, so that by the time they reach a house or office they should still be clean and protected for a while.

However, pests do appear on house plants and there are a few which are more common than others and we should keep an eye open for them as an infected plant will never thrive and will pass its pests on to other plants in the locality.

Aphids, usually greenfly, which affect roses and other garden plants, can waft through an open window or be brought indoors on cut flowers. Unfortunately these breed so quickly that often between the time of one watering-cum-inspection and another the plant can become well and truly infested.

Keep a look out, then, especially during the summer months, for aphids. Look for any hint of a change in the habit or appearance of a plant. A sure sign of distress is the sudden yellowing of leaves. Study them, with a magnifying glass if necessary, and if aphids are the cause of the trouble you will see the tiny insects on the undersides and on the growing tips of the stems. A sticky film on some leaves, and sometimes also on windowsills or furniture, will also indicate the presence of aphids.

Prompt action is essential. You can spray the plant with any good insecticide, but always take the plant outside to do this. Remember that all insecticides are poisons and should never be splashed about in the confined air of the home. The most simple treatment is to take precautions and use a systemic insecticide soon after the plant comes into your possession, so that if and when an insect comes along and sucks at the sap of a plant it is killed before it has an opportunity to increase its numbers.

Systemic insecticides can be watered into the soil and will gradually pass up through the roots into the sap in the stems and leaves. As the pests are sucking insects they soon become affected. It takes time for this type of insecticide to enter the system of a plant, so it is not a first aid measure for an already infected plant.

Sometimes it is cheaper, quicker and safer to throw out the plant, clean the containers and the area in which the plant was growing and begin again. Check first on such matters as the rarity or cost of the plant, the degree of infestation, the difficulty of treatment and similar matters before making up your mind. Remember, however, that insect attack is comparatively rare for most house plants.

I am hoping to be able to persuade the reader that routine is both possible and to be recommended, and this particular problem is a case in point. During the summer months include a dose of systemic insecticide in the watering of those house plants most prone to aphid attack. There are types of modern systemics which are suitable for all types of plants.

Sometimes, a seemingly healthy plant will suddenly succumb and appear to be dried and shrivelled. This is when it is attacked by a tiny mite known as red spider, so small that it is almost impossible to detect with the naked eye. The first indications that there is something wrong will be an unusual leaf fall, distorted leaves, twisted shoots or a rusty tinge to the plant, or a sudden glimpse of what appear to be cobwebs over some of the leaves and growing stems. It is these webs that have given the red spider mite its incorrect name. It is a difficult pest to eradicate indoors and it will spread to other plants. It comes when conditions are too dry and arid, another case for providing humidity at all times. It is best in cases of a severe attack to throw out the plant and wait a while before introducing the same type again.

On the other hand, if the plant is small in size and can be conveniently handled, it may be possible to effect a cure by dipping the entire plant, pot included, into a bucket containing a solution of white oils, obtainable from garden shops.

There are only two other real pests which are likely to

appear from time to time. One is mealy bug, which appears almost like a piece of sticky cotton wool on a leaf or joint. It can be scraped away with a matchstick or twig dipped in white oils or methylated spirits. Once it appears on a plant keep a regular look out for it, because it is sometimes difficult to see and one piece may have been overlooked during your treatment.

Scale is to be found on only a few plants and it is difficult to remove. It looks like a tiny shell sticking firmly to a leaf or sometimes like a very small wood louse. It must be prised off and the uncovered area painted with a little white oils.

There is yet another factor which will cause leaves to turn yellow and a house plant ultimately to die, and this is unclean air. In some cases even the smallest amount of domestic gas in the atmosphere, perhaps from a cooker some distance away in another room, will have its effect. Fumes from oil heaters, coke, petrol or traffic fumes, even tobacco, have all been known to kill some sensitive plants.

I have seen plants growing in a kitchen where there is gas, but very few actually thrive under these conditions. Some tough characters, such as aspidistras, will go on growing in a house in which one might think that the air was too polluted to sustain plant life, but in the main it would be wiser, I believe, to forget trying to grow certain plants under these conditions. The alternative is to specialise in Wardian cases and bottle gardens, where plants grow encased in their own clean micro-climate.

2. The Easiest of All

It is many years now since I first began indoor gardening and right back in the early days I was given a handsome plant which looked far too strange and exotic ever to grow in my London office. It was *Aechmea rhodocyanea* and it did grow – splendidly!

There are still aechmeas in my home, though they now enjoy the clean country air and they are all descendants of that first plant. Through the years they have increased in numbers and I have had plenty to pass on to other indoor gardeners, something I do with confidence, for the aechmea is a plant I would heartily recommend to anyone who wants to begin growing house plants. My experience has proved to me that it surely is one of the easiest of all to grow.

First, an explanation of the name. The generic name comes from *aichme*, a point. This is a reference to the sharply pointed calyx which gives the flower spike, inflorescence or scape – call it what you will – its characteristic shape, appearance and texture. And the specific name, *rhodocyanea,* simply means rose-blue.

Actually the flower stem is a fascinating and gorgeous growth. It rises from the centre of the plant, a wonderful magenta-pink spike, finally towering above the handsome, curving, grey-green foliage. It then expands displaying those stiff, pointed calyces which give the plant its name. These protect the blue, violet and rose florets which stud the stem like jewels. A further bonus is that the scape is very long lived. It will remain fresh and flower studded for about three months, and even after it has really faded it will still be too attractive for you to want to cut it away.

The aechmea has another, simpler, folk or common name,

24

the Greek vase plant, a reference to its shape and character-istic manner of growth. Here lies its success as a house plant for beginners! Because it is a 'vase' the aechmea offers abso-lutely no problems so far as watering is concerned. The lower portion of the leaves wrap closely around each other and form a funnel, vase or cup, and all you, as an aechmea owner, have to do is to keep this vase topped up with water at all times.

You can forget about soil conditions, the roots and all those wonderful scientific facts which I gave you about aeration in the previous chapter so far as this plant is concerned. Aechmea is a true individualist.

Earlier I said that our house plants are drawn from many sections of the plant world. Aechmea is one of the tribe Bromeliaceae. Collectively these plants are called bromeliads. They are all very interesting botanically. Many of them are epiphytic, which means that they are plants which grow not on the ground but on another plant, usually a tree. They do not draw nourishment from the host plant and so are not para-sitic like the mistletoe, but are merely anchored in it. Epiphytes are most abundant in tropical regions, where the environment offers a uniformly high temperature coupled with a high humidity.

In these areas there is great competition among plants all striving for a share of light and moisture. Where there is a dense layer of foliage overhead, unless they have become evolved and adapted to make the most of such a situation the plants on lower levels may not receive a full share of rainfall and thus become denied essential moisture.

Many epiphytes have specially constructed roots which en-able them both to condense and to absorb the moisture pre-sent in the atmosphere instead of having to search for it in the soil. Indeed, some are given the name of air plants because they may seem to live on air alone. Others have specially structured leaves which prevent water from escaping, or can conserve it in some way. This our aechmea does. Any tiny drop of moisture is conveyed by some means or another down into the central funnel.

Soil is not of great significance to an aechmea. It needs only sufficient to give it anchorage. Yet what soil there is should be open and well drained. The soil-less composts suit it well. Trained gardeners of the old school used equal parts of leaf-mould, peat and good loam, with a generous sprinkling of sharp sand to keep the compost porous. And even then, first they placed a good layer of drainage crocks, usually broken clay flower pots, on the base and covered these with a layer of moss.

Neither does the aechmea require much water, except at times when it is at the peak of its growth or is sending up a flower spike. This being the case, you can see that we would be wasting our time to make it grow like all the other terrestial types.

Because of this, aechmeas are usually grown and marketed in pots which are comparatively small for the size of the plant. And as these pots are usually plastic and consequently light in weight, the plant tends to be top heavy and constantly being knocked over.

Here plunging comes into its own. As a cover pot I like to choose a tall, heavy container, usually a pedestal vase normally used for flowers, which I think adds grace to the plant, especially when it is in flower and several inches taller overall.

In spite of the fact that the aechmea roots do not require much water for most of the time I keep the plunge medium uniformly moist, thus ensuring that the leaves grow in humid air. And I like to think that the peat which surrounds the roots in the pot is not so very different from the decaying rubbish of a tropical jungle caught in some crevice in a tree, in which one imagines epiphytes germinate in the first place.

My aechmea first stood in a sunny window because I read that the plants must have light, yet others I have had have flowered just as well in a fireplace well back in a room and even in a north aspect, which shows how tolerant it is to differing light conditions. This plant will also withstand a wide variation of temperatures.

Americans, who can claim the aechmea as a native plant along with many more of the same tribe, call those which are domesticated room pines. This name has no connection with trees which bear cones, but is an acknowledgement of the fact that the pineapple belongs to the same tribe and that some of the bromeliads do look like pineapple plants.

It is possible to grow pineapples, or ananas, the South American name for this plant, indoors, where often they will even bear fruit. There is a beautifully decorative variety of *Ananas comosus* with spiny foliage variegated with tints of ruby and the palest pink, with cream and soft greens. This can bring a distinctive touch of colour in a room, but it must be grown in a warm, draught-free home.

A plant can be propagated from the green topknot of leaves on a pineapple, so long as the heart of the shoot has not been removed, as it sometimes is before export. But before I describe how to do this, may I say a little about other bromeliads which can be found on sale and which are not too difficult for the indoor gardener who can offer the plants a warm home.

Cryptanthus are an interesting and usually coloured group. *C. acaulis* (the specific name means without stalks or seeming to be without stalks) resembles the aechmea more than others you may see. *C. bromelioides tricolor* has coloration very similar to the pineapple described above. Although it also is tolerant about the light it receives, it is only fair to say that it will produce its most intense colours when grown in good light.

The leaves of some of the smaller species do not always form such distinctively shaped 'vases' as the aechmea, but are instead star-shaped. One name for them is earth stars. Even so, there is still a well in the centre which should be kept constantly moist. These plants need a little more water on the soil, easily given by over-filling the vase a little at each watering so that the excess trickles through on to the soil surface.

An attractive way to display a collection of these plants and to keep them happy at the same time is to fasten them on to a tree made from a well anchored branch or piece of driftwood on which sphagnum moss has been bound with string or wire. Bury the pots or plant the roots in the moss and keep it and the plant centres well sprayed with clean water at all times. One friend of mine nailed his plants, through the roots, to the wood! I understand they lasted well!

Another tough house bromeliad, almost garden-hardy in fact, is *Billbergia nutans*. J. G. Billberg was a botanist, and nutans means nodding or drooping, a reference to the flowers on their long stalk. This plant has slightly spined leaves, reminiscent of, though thinner than, the pineapple. Its blooms are fabulous and if you have sufficient plant space it is worth growing the plant for these alone. Out of flower the billbergia is not particularly decorative, and unfortunately the flowers are nothing like so long lived as those of the aechmea. One way to prolong the flowering season is to keep the plant in a cool place, a north window for example.

But to return to our aechmea. When the plant has finished flowering it begins to increase by producing suckers or offsets near its base in the pot, looking like tiny plants themselves. Sometimes there may be only one, sometimes there are three, four or five. As these mature the parent plant dies.

You can leave these daughter plants as they are and allow them to grow on in the same pot to form a multiple plant, but this way then tend to occupy too wide an area and to become a nuisance. It is usually more practical to detach them from the parent plant and grow them on as individuals. This way we propagate the plant vegetatively, not from seed but from suckers or offsets. There are other plants which can be increased in the same way.

The first one we tackled in our home had three daughter plants and we had allowed them to grow to a good size before it was decided that the plant would be better divided. When it was tipped out of its pot it became obvious that the root ball was extremely fibrous and tough. When one divides some other types of plants it is usually quite easy merely to pull the roots apart at obvious division points. In the case of this aechmea a sharp knife was necessary. The root was cut into three so that each offset had a good portion to itself. These roots were then tidied and teased so that stray wisps and severed portions, not really attached to anything, were pulled away. The daughter plants were each potted individually and we had no more trouble. This is the method I continue to use.

I have read that the correct way to take aechmea and other bromeliad suckers or offsets is first to cut them from the plant, to strip away some of the lower leaves and trim the base (this is said to help form a callus, which is inducive to root formation) and after this to pot each one in sandy soil and stand them in moist heat.

Moist heat is the kind generated in a hothouse, sometimes called a stove house. It is not easy for an amateur indoor gardener to provide, demanding considerable heat and humidity

Callusing helps a pineapple tuft to root. First make sure that it is young and healthy and then cut it away with as little of the fruit flesh as possible. Strip the lowest leaf or two and trim the base to remove loose pieces of skin and other vegetation. Now lie the tuft down somewhere so that the air will dry the cut base. After a couple of days pot it into a mixture of moist peat and sand. It must be kept really warm and humid or it will not root. Slip the pot and cutting inside a clear plastic bag large enough to envelop both without touching the leaves. Blow into the bag to inflate it if necessary. Close it tight to keep it airtight. Examine the cutting after two weeks or so, and when the roots are growing well move it into a potting compost. Later, when your plant is well grown, it can be increased again from offsets or suckers.

There are a number of other bromeliads which are both as easy to grow and as rewarding as those mentioned previously, but I have not drawn special attention to them simply because they are not always easy to find in our shops and markets.

Neoregelia carolinae 'tricolor' has long, saw-toothed leaves streaked green and cream, and meeting in the centre in the characteristic vase. Although the flower it produces is insignificant, the interesting and attractive thing about this plant is that shortly before the flower appears the central vase begins to blush, a first a delicate pink and then a fiery scarlet just before the flowers appear.

Much the same blushing habit is also shown by *Nidularium marechati,* which has somewhat wider and blunter foliage of deep green. The centre again turns a vivid scarlet when the flowers are about to appear.

B

Another bromeliad, *Tillandsia lindeniana,* tends to reverse things, for here the plant itself is somewhat insignificant, with narrow, toothed and untidy leaves of dull green, but it produces a tall flower stalk surmounted by a scape holding many beautiful blue flowers in the centre of a series of pink bracts, long lasting.

Vriesia fenestralis and *V. hieroglyphica* both have unimportant flowers but long, smooth, regular strap-like leaves with the most beautiful markings. The basic colour is a deep grey-green and the markings are in green, grey, chocolate brown, purple or mauve.

These latter plants are well worth growing and if an example is found it should be grabbed, for young plants are easily propagated by taking the offsets.

3. Some Relatives of the Fig

The rubber plant, *Ficus elastica* 'Decora' is probably one of the best known of all our house plants. It seems so much at home in today's scene, flaunting its distinctive shape and thick leathery foliage in a thousand photographs of modern interiors that it comes as something of a surprise to read a Victorian reporter, a Mr Charles Dickens, grumbling about seeing the plant all over the place, in every parlour window!

As the Royal Horticultural Society's Dictionary of Gardening so concisely and truly states, "it stands confinement in rooms exceedingly well", which no doubt is the reason why it has been a plant pet for such a long time.

I have chosen it as an example for a chapter of this book for several reasons, which I hope to make clear, but mainly because it really is such a good plant for a beginner.

It may surprise the reader to learn that the rubber plant and the delicious fig are related. The mulberry also is a cousin not very far removed. But the rubber plant is not the only ficus grown as a house plant. There are others, some also with large leaves, others with small foliage and daintier appearance.

Left to grow naturally, *Ficus elastica* becomes a branching tree in its native environment, up to 100 feet tall, yet *F. pumila* is a small-leaved climber, a clinging type, which will cover a wall in a greenhouse or conservatory, or even a garden room if sufficient humidity can be provided. This species, unlike most other house plants, is almost garden-hardy and can actually be grown outside in warm areas. It offers advantages to those wishing to decorate places which can be kept only just above freezing point. There is a pretty variegated type confusingly known as *F. scandens* when it should be *F. pumila* 'Variegata'. This one is just a little more tender, needing more

31

light and sun. *F. benjamina,* a favourite house plant with many, more resembles a neat citrus tree. Like many of the figs it does not conform to a recognisable habit. This one is a real individualist. In its native habitat it becomes epiphytic in its old age!

There are, in fact, more than 600 species of ficus, only comparatively few of which are grown as house plants. No doubt we shall see more grown indoors as time passes and they prove their worth. In some cases I expect that we shall grow varieties of them rather than the species themselves.

If you are puzzled over the meaning of botanical terms, perhaps a short explanation will be helpful.

The first part of a plant name is the generic term and it denotes the plant's tribe. It is the plant's surname in a way. Through it you can discover relationships, sometimes with surprise, for without knowing the genera you might never have suspected that two widely differing plants were related. The second part of the name is the specific term and tells us something of the character, habit or origin of the plant, a little like the charming Welsh custom of calling, for example, the local baker Jones the Bread, so that one knows something about the man immediately. So, in this case, we have *Ficus,* an old latin name for the fig, and *elastica,* a reference to the milky sap or latex from which rubber is produced and for which commercially grown trees are tapped.

(If you cut or damage a ficus in some way you will soon see the white sap oozing from the wound. It is as well to stop this flow as quickly as you can. I usually simply drop a pinch of dry soil, sand, or even Florapak or Oasis from my flower arrangements, on the wound to stem the sap so that it will coagulate quickly.)

A species gives rise from seed to others identical in every way to itself, but occasionally a stranger appears in a batch of seedlings. Perhaps the plant is identical in every other way except that its leaves are variegated. Usually when a variegated form arises it is given an extra piece to its name and is known as, say, *Ficus elastica* 'Variegata', and we say that it is a variegated variety or form. Sometimes though the difference does not lie in variegation. There may be different colouring, the plant may be more vigorous or be of a more endearing habit. Such a variety is often given the name of a person, but sometimes the term is merely descriptive. And because it has become the variety's name it is written like a proper noun, *Ficus elastica* 'Decora'.

Decora was a seedling which was grown on a nursery and which was such an improvement on its parent that it soon superseded the species. There are other varieties of *F. elastica* on sale in different parts of the world. I know that many people like to give homely names to plants, but these do cause confusion, especially, as sometimes happens, when the same name may be used in another part of the country to describe a completely different plant.

I find it exasperating when I cannot answer a reader's query because the name used is made up and unknown to me, and there is no way I can trace it.

Even while they say that they prefer pretty folk names, many people use a great many more botanical names than they realise. They have no objection, for example, to using aspidistra, aubrieta, geranium, hydrangea, alyssum, aster or viola to mention only a few, simply because these have become familiar. So it seems a pity to me that they don't try to become at home with others. On the other hand, many people use a plant's specific term as its real name. Think, for example again, of the number who call chaenomeles or ornamental quince, 'japonica'. Yet this term simply means that the plant originated in Japan and the same specific term is given to many other quite different plants from that country.

So I make no excuse for using a plant's real name. I prefer it. And should I wish to talk about plants to gardeners in any other part of the world, or should they read this book, we shall both understand each other, for botanical nomenclature has been specially designed to be international.

But to return to our figs! There are few plain *Ficus elastica* on sale today, for most have been superseded by the variety Decora, which has larger, broader, heavier leaves which sport a nice touch of crimson on the midrib on the undersides of the leaves and in the sheath on the growing tips. And a variegated form exists in *F. elastica* 'Decora' – 'Schrijvereana', a Belgian raised variety. This, though extremely handsome, is a little more difficult to grow, so wait a while before bringing it into your home if you are a new indoor gardener.

Ficus elastica could not have become so popular and so well known if it had not been so tolerant. When one considers its origins it is really surprising that it has done so well for such a long time. Consider, that when it was first popular, the air in a home was nothing like so clean as it is now, for there were candles, oil lamps, gas, fires, smoke and fog.

It comes from tropical Asia, a jungle plant, which means that it grows naturally under shady, even gloomy conditions. Its dark green, leathery leaves are an indication of this. Take our only native example, not a plant from the same family but one which also often has to grow below other trees and creepers, the wild ivy. Just think how dark and how tough are its leaves.

Here, then, is a splendid object lesson for the beginner gardener. The darker green and the thicker its leaves the less light a plant needs, for both these things denote a shady character.

So this ficus is a plant for the hall or for the corner of a room rather than to stand in a sunny window, although it will survive even here. However, when it does so, to the experienced eye the leaves always look slightly 'tanned', though not discoloured.

Thick leaves have another characteristic. They are long-lived and must be treated with great care. Should it lose some of its leaves a ficus is not equipped as are some other plants quickly to produce new foliage. The stem remains bereft and the plant loses much of its beauty. Leaves can become damaged and will fall should the plant be stood in such a place that it becomes frequently brushed as someone passes by. So it is important to take care when you decide where a plant is to stand. A ficus will also lose leaves from other causes, as I will explain later.

These large, thick leaves which hang around for so long, sometimes for years, become dusty unless they are regularly cleaned. Unfortunately it is (or so it sometimes seems to me) the desire of many plant owners to have plant foliage gleaming as brightly as their waxed floors and furniture. The poor ficus suffers many indignities and hurts in this respect. Often I have been proudly told of leaves which are kept gleaming by being sponged with milk, smoothed with vaseline, lubricated with olive oil and then the proud owner wonders why, ultimately, they fall long before their time. No special unguents are necessary. Oils and grease clog the pores until the leaf can no longer function properly. It turns yellow and falls.

Leaves are the lungs of a plant. Through the pores in them a plant breathes. It also loses water through them too. They are essential orifices and must be kept free of dust and any other matter that might tend to clog them. Outdoors, wind, rain and dew help to keep foliage clean. Indoors, we have to take other measures. One must avoid scratching the leaf surface with dust as it is removed, something which is so easy to do. Much depends upon where the plant lives. If there is no likelihood of walls or furniture becoming spoiled one can spray leaves regularly with clean water from a spray or atomiser which makes a fine, gentle mist. On some of my large-leaved house plants I frequently use the vacuum cleaner with the soft dusting brush attached.

When I lived in London I was constantly concerned about the amount of grit which settled on the leaves of most of my plants, especially during the winter months. Once the weather had turned warm I used to line the bath with an old sheet so that it would not become scratched and then take what plants could be carried into the bathroom there to spring clean them with a hand shower and tepid water. It was surprising to see just how much dirt was washed from them this way.

It is well worth while collecting rain water both to water and to spray the plants. However, that which is collected in industrial areas is not always clean. It may be black with soot brought down off the roofs and may also contain sulphur and other impurities, so it should not be used. But where rain water is clean use it regularly to spray the plants, even taking them outdoors where this is possible. Remember that regular spraying with clean water is also a good means of keeping down insect pests and of increasing supplies of humidity.

Incidentally, it may be that the plant itself is wet enough at the roots, and if the spray water is allowed to wash down into the soil this might make it too sodden. Should this be the case enclose the pot in a plastic bag, drawing the neck up close to the main stem.

It is quite all right to stand house plants outdoors in a shower, but you must be certain that the rain is warm and not cold or icy, and also that the plant is well anchored and not likely to become blown over or damaged.

An unhappy ficus will soon show signs of distress by the angle at which it hangs its leaves. When it is well these are almost at right angles to the main stem, with young plants pointing their leaves very slightly upwards and more mature plants pointing them very slightly downwards. But a thirsty plant, and perversely one which is too wet, will point its leaves even further to the roots as if indicating that it is down there that the trouble lies.

I have always found it surprising that so many people find it hard to tell when soil is dry. Obviously, being able to tell with only a cursory glance can only come with experience, but it surely is such a simple matter to lift a pot and weigh it in the hand. Dry soil is very light and that which is newly watered quite heavy.

As I said earlier, it is almost impossible to give precise instructions on how frequently a plant should be watered. So far as a *Ficus elastica* is concerned so much will depend upon the climate of the room in which it grows. And there is another thing to consider : those thick, tough leaves do not give up their moisture readily. Loss from them is much slower than from a plant whose leaves are soft and sappy.

In winter, growth is slower and generally the plant will need much less water than it requires in summer. In a cool home one might be able to go as long as two, three or even four weeks before watering again. But in a warm house, even though a plant may not be drawing on the reserves of water for its new growth, the moisture from the soil or the plunge medium around the pot continues to evaporate, sometimes quite fast. In a warm home in winter a weekly drink may be necessary.

Quite often the soil surface indicates the water content. While this is damp below, the surface remains dark in hue. As the soil dries a whitish crust is formed on the surface. When this occurs it is time to water.

Sometimes the symptoms of over-watering are not immediately obvious. A ficus may appear to be going along quite nicely. One knows that it is receiving exactly the same treatment as always. And then, suddenly, a leaf will turn yellow and you wonder what it is that you have recently done wrong. It might be helpful to think back. You may have gone on holiday and asked a friend or neighbour to water your plants. Or there may have been a power cut, a cooler house than usual, yet you continued with the same watering routine.

A cold draught will also cause leaves to drop, and not only the leaves of a ficus. As I write, only this morning I heard from a reader asking what had happened to her ficus which she had had for such a long time. She had recently moved house and in its new home three of its leaves had turned yellow and dropped. The cause of the trouble was revealed in her postscript. "In my old house I used electricity and here I have gas heating in my room. Would this make any difference?" It would, and unfortunately it had.

As the ficus grows naturally in the open and its branches spread out to a great size, its stem grows and thickens too until finally it becomes the bare trunk of the tree with a beauty all its own. But a pot plant, which after all in this case is really only a rooted cutting, does not look at all attractive with the lower part of its stem bare of leaves.

"What can I do about it?" I am so often asked. "Will the tip root if I cut it off and re-pot it?"

Yes, it will root. You can begin all over again and make a 'new' plant, but the tip must not be severed from its stem until it has made roots of its own and is capable of caring adequately for itself.

This introduces us to a fascinating process known as air

layering. What we have to do is to encourage other roots to grow while the old roots are still in the pot. To do this, using a sharp knife, care and patience and only just cutting through the skin of the stem, mark a circle right around the stem at a point about nine inches from the lowest leaf. Mark another circle about half an inch lower down and then remove the bark between the cuts. This peeled or naked portion of the stem must now be covered. Have ready a good wad of moist sphagnum moss, a little larger than a tennis ball. If you can't get this from a florist or a garden centre, use well soaked Oasis, a foamed plastic normally used to hold stems in place in flower arrangements, and on sale at all florist shops and some department stores in blocks and small cylinders.

If you cut a cylinder down through the centre you will be able to press both sides together against the stem quite easily. The stem will make its indentation so that the wound is safely covered.

Roots will grow from this cut area into the moist medium surrounding it so long as it is covered so that little or no evaporation takes place. The best method is to use a piece of clear plastic sheeting and completely envelop the moss or Oasis, taking it both up and down the stem a little way. Gather it in and tie it firmly to the stem at top and bottom.

New roots will grow into the moss or other medium after a few weeks. You will be able to see through the plastic covering and when the roots are obviously well grown the new plant can be severed from the naked stem and potted up in the usual way.

If you find that the roots are holding right to the rooting medium do not try to pull them away, simply pot the whole ball in good compost. Water and leave until the soil is almost dry again before starting the regular routine.

4. Some Unexpected Lilies

When I look at the neat, shining, variegated leaves of the pretty chlorophytum I must confess to being puzzled over the interpretation of its botanical name, *chloros,* meaning green and *phyton,* a plant! Someone must have run out of original ideas! Neither term tells us anything at all about a distinctive and ornamental plant which was so admired for its decorative value by the Victorians that one person at least is recorded as having had holes made in her grand dining table, so that the pots could be sunk to their rims, leaving only the neat tufts of leaves to rise from its polished surface.

The *R.H.S. Dictionary of Gardening* dismisses the chlorophytum somewhat brusquely, it seems to me: "Of little horticultural value but *C. elatum variegatum* is frequently grown in greenhouses and rooms for its white-striped foliage." And so it is.

As you would expect, those plants in greenhouses seem more at ease than those in a home, simply because there they can be grown in a really humid atmosphere. The biggest plant I ever saw was suspended from a greenhouse roof and grew in a moss-lined hanging basket. Instead of cascading in the characteristic manner downwards from the centre of the plant, its runners or stolons had grown into the damp, mossy surface of the basket until the whole formed a great globe of tufts of prettily striped leaves.

Just what the dictionary means by "of little horticultural value" I am not sure, and certainly not in agreement, because I know that this plant is highly valued by a great many people up and down the land who have found it a delightful and easy thing to grow.

It is of value to me at the moment for the purposes of

this book as it gives me the opportunity to introduce with it some of the other plants of its own tribe which also make good house plants.

But first a longer look at the chlorophytum itself. And before I begin I must apologise in advance for the nomenclature, for here we are beset with the vexed subject of the use of synonyms.

Synonyms occur, so I am told, because when a plant is first discovered it is named in good faith for the first time. Later someone finds out that instead of the plant being a complete newcomer as was thought, actually someone else, perhaps in some other part of the world, already knew of it and indeed had even named it and placed his name for it on record. There has been a great move in the past decade or two to tidy the world's plant nomenclature, but we are still often stuck with more than one name for one species. *C. elatum,* which means stately, has another name, *C. capense,* which simply means that it comes from the Cape.

But this plant has been superseded commercially by another, *C. comosum,* a superior species from the decorative point of view. This in turn has produced some fine varieties and it is one of these that you are most likely to find on sale. I would advise you not to worry unduly about the correct name, for the mode of cultivation is the same for any and all.

Generally speaking *elatum* is out and in its place the specific term *capense,* and, though incorrectly, even *comosum* are used. The beginner who prefers common names will, I am sure, prefer to call them all spider plant, the homely name given originally to *C. elatum vittatum*!

One can see how such a plant came to be called a spider, for there is a resemblance, both in the outline of a single young plant and one which is mature. An older plant develops arching stems on which little white flowers, really tiny lilies, grow in racemes. Later on the tips of these flowering stems tiny plantlets or stolons are formed, altogether an entertaining and engaging habit.

This method of growth is different from that of most other house plants. The only other one similar which I can recall at

the moment is the little *Saxifraga sarmentosa,* sometimes called
Mother of Thousands because of the many plantlets it produces
on long stolons as thin as thread. In its case though the flower
stems grow from the centres of the rosettes of leaves in the
more usual way of plants.

Chlorophytums are seldom seen at their best in many homes,
where they are expected to remain compact, upright and neat.
But this is not the nature of the plant. I am surprised that we
do not see more growing in hanging baskets indoors, in a window for example. They fill this role admirably. In summer the
baskets can be hung outside. Incidentally, chlorophytums are
often an ingredient of a summer hanging basket of mixed
plants, both flowering and foliage types.

I have a tall iron lamp stand, originally designed to hold
an oil lamp aloft, and this displays a chlorophytum beautifully.
The plant I have is many years old and has been a source of
dozens of plants which have been passed on to friends. Its pot
fits into the well meant for the lamp. Here the plant has space
to spread its leaves. The stolons can and do reach down as far
as they like. When it is growing well there are two or three
dozen of them each dangling a tuft of little leaves, promises of
new plants. It makes an effective and attractive room decoration.

In one over-tidy home I once saw three poor chlorophytum
on a windowsill, each staked and tied tightly to a cane, stolons
and all. They made a poor picture and not in the least decorative.

Yet this is such an easy and rewarding plant. The long
leaves, grass-like in appearance, are either green and white
or cream, or light yellow and green, the paler colour making
a band down the centre. It grows under almost any conditions,
although if it is not happy for some reason or other the tips
of the leaves tend to turn brown. But as they do this anyway
before they fade away from old age, one can too easily become
concerned for no real reason. Some people trim the brown
leaf ends to a new point with scissors.

The plant also likes plenty of water in summer, when it
should also be fed from time to time, and less in winter. It

will grow in a sunny window or in shade, in a hot room or in one which is just above freezing point. All that it asks is that the treatment it receives is sensitively adjusted to its environment. This means, of course, that it will require more water, and perhaps even a little spraying of the air around it to promote a humid atmosphere in hot and dry conditions, and less if it is grown elsewhere. Plants in cool rooms often need very little water in winter.

I am never without new plants simply because it is such a simple matter to propagate them. Those little plantlets proffered so freely will soon root in water, moist sand, soil or potting and seed composts. Indeed, some of them start growing their rather thick and succulent roots while they are still in mid air dangling from the plant.

Some people prefer to layer them, guiding each plantlet on to the surface of a pot of soil and anchoring it there so that the roots grow. When this has happened the plant is detached from its parent by the simple process of cutting through the linking stem. *C. comosum* and its varieties produce plantlets more freely than does *capense,* perhaps another reason why the first has superseded the second.

When the plant flowers it may be hard to realise that those tiny petalled stars which stud the long stem really are lilies, but if you examine them closely you will see the family likeness, the floral pattern of three on three.

One of the really fascinating things about plant families is the great difference in appearance that often exists between one member and another. Who, for example, would think that the yellow buttercup and the tall blue delphinium were cousins?

All plants in the Liliaceae have parallel veins running lengthwise from stem end to leaf tip. This is because they belong to one of the two great groups of flowering plants known as Monocotyledons, all members of which produce only one seed leaf or cotyledon when the seed germinates. Grass is an example. In the other great division, Dicotyledons, two seed leaves are produced. Mustard and cress are examples here.

So, since things are not always what they may first appear to be, who would think that old-timer the aspidistra was cousin to the madonna lily? Its flowers are less like a lily's than anything you can imagine. They are strange, pinkish growths which appear on the soil surface at the foot of the long, tough leaves. They give the plant its name, *aspidiseon,* a small round shield.

Here, too, is a good-tempered, tolerant and adaptable plant which, in fact, once grew so well under appalling home conditions before the days of electricity that people became contemptuous of it and threw it out. It is now fashionable again, but harder to find!

Here too is a plant not often enough seen at its splendid best. If you grow aspidistras in a good compost and never allow the roots to become too dry you will come to own some really handsome plants. If these are fed occasionally with doses of liquid plant food the leaf texture will become a glossy dark green.

As with chlorophytum, you can divide a large plant. My mother passed one on to me which she had had ever since I can remember and at the time she gave it to me it certainly wasn't all that beautiful. Its leaves were small and looked stunted and starved. It was knocked from its pot and the mass of roots were gradually teased apart and we found more than forty separate crowns or plants. Each one was then potted separately and most were given away, but I saved three for myself and these now are really ornamental. They little resemble their undernourished and ancient parent plant.

If you do not wish to go to the trouble of turning a healthy plant out of its pot to divide in order to get an extra plant, you can cut suckers from the parent plant and pot these. These are leaves which have grown up a little distance from the crown of the plant. See that each has a portion of root adhering. The best way is first to scratch away gently some of the soil from around the leaf until you can tell that you will be able to cut through a piece of root. Do this with a sharp knife. Replace the soil.

It is possible sometimes to buy a variegated aspidistra, *A. elatior* 'Variegata'. If you see one, snap it up, for these are almost collector's pieces. Like many other variegated forms of plants it is perhaps not quite so robust as the green type. If you can grow it well enough to warrant division you should have some fine plants to give away as special presents.

'Ferns' are not always what they seem. Many people are under the impression that the asparagus fern, *Asparagus plumosus,* is a true fern, but this is not so. Once again it is a member of the lily family, and is in fact a berry-bearing, slightly prickly, evergreen climber. It is a direct cousin of *A. officinalis,* the delicious vegetable asparagus, which are the young shoots of a tall, plumosus-like plant. The name asparagus is an old Greek one.

There are many kinds of asparagus fern in cultivation, including the dwarf compactus and nanus. There are also many other species usually grown in greenhouses. These include *A. sprengeri,* once such a popular component of bouquets and flower arrangements and its varieties. The thornless smilax, or *A. medeoloides,* and its varieties so beloved by Victorian decorators is another which was often seen draped in generous swags on snowy damask dinner tables.

A. plumosus is easy to grow and indeed will live for years and years if it finds its home, and yours, to its liking. It dislikes heat, direct sunshine and draughts, either hot or cold. I grow my own plant in a north facing window in a well lighted room which has a fairly even temperature the year round, which are perfect conditions for this particular plant.

It came to me in a gift bowl with a variegated ivy, *Hedera canariensis,* and a poinsettia. The latter was removed and in its place I planted a plectranthus which scrambles attractively over the rim of the bowl. Surprisingly, the asparagus has continued to grow in spite of the fact that the bowl is plastic and only some nine inches wide and two deep.

I like to keep the foliage sprayed during the summer when the air is dry. I am certain then that this is being cleaned. These plants need quite a lot of water in the summer. At the same time they should be fed once a month with a liquid plant food. During the winter one must use one's discretion, and when the plant is making no new growth the food should be withheld.

You can raise *A. plumosus* from seed on a warm and sunny window sill. A large plant can be divided but this is not so easy, nor is it always successful, because the roots are often difficult to divide as they are so matted.

Quite different in appearance and extremely handsome is the sansevieria, named in honour of eighteenth-century Raimondo di Sangro, Prince of Sansevero, in Southern Italy. The tall, sharp, sword-like leaves of this plant have earned it the unkind name of Mother-in-law's tongue. There are actually more than 50 species, but not all are house plants. Most frequently seen is *S. trifasciata* and its varieties and cultivars. Of these *S. t. laurentii* is most often seen on sale.

This couldn't be a more adaptable or agreeable plant. I have seen sansevierias growing under all possible conditions and many of these quite unconducive to growth, or so one would think. The tall leaves are a dark green, mottled, striped and banded with grey-greens and yellow.

The plant grows from a creeping rhizome, a thick, wandering underground stem from which it will, if it likes the conditions you have provided, throw up one or more new leaves each year until the pot is really full. Such plants can be very handsome. If you wish a large plant can be divided up to make two or more smaller specimens. Use the same method as for an aspidistra.

A mature plant will sometimes produce greenish-white flowers growing in a loose raceme rising from the base of the leaves. These are wonderfully and powerfully fragrant, their scent being strongest at night.

Although a sansevieria is not actually a succulent I like to treat it as one. The thick leaves store moisture for long periods. In winter the soil should be kept almost dry, which means applying water (and then only a little) about once a month, depending of course on the relative humidity and warmth of your home. One should water more frequently in summer, weekly perhaps, and feed about once a month during this time.

You may possibly see other types of sansevieria on sale, including the shorter, stockier, 'bird's nest' sansevieria, *S. hahnii*.

Once you have grown one type well you should have no difficulty in growing another.

Some people call the sansevieria the lizard plant because of its markings. Personally I don't think that the name is really apt, although I must admit to a comparatively sketchy experience of lizard life. However, I do approve of the name partridge plant for another member of the lily family, *Aloe variegata*. This, a favourite for cottage windows, is a true succulent. Many kinds can be found in the lily tribe, but not all are suitable as house plants. This one will grow in the shade.

It is a beautiful plant with chunky, triangular, blue-green leaves, zigzagged with white markings which resemble those on the breast of the bird after which the plant is named. The flowers, too, are attractive; tubular, a coral red, set in a loose raceme which gradually expands to tower above the formal cluster of leaves.

There are many aloes but few are easy to find or to buy. Some of them are spiny, unlike the partridge plant in appearance and more resembling a pineapple top.

Propagation for *Aloe variegata* is again by means of offsets. You can also raise it from seed.

All like a sunny position and a fairly warm and even temperature. Water them only about once a month in winter and more frequently from April to August. If the soil is allowed to remain too wet for too long the plant may die, its roots rotting in the damp soil. Make sure, if you repot, which is best done every two or three years with a well grown plant, that the soil is really well drained. If you use a bought compost a good tip is to fill one third of the pot first with small nuggets of charcoal. I have more to say about caring for succulents in a later chapter.

Aloes, like some other house plants, are sometimes attacked by both scale insects and mealy bugs. The first, which looks like a Lilliputian mussel shell clinging to the surface of the leaf, is best removed by hand. The second is more difficult to eradicate, for it sometimes nestles right in the heart of a plant, between the spines when these are present, or in the leaf axils, according to the type of plant affected. In appearance it resembles a spot of cotton wool.

Derris dust is a good controller. Blow this into the heart of the plant and leave it for a few days. Alternatively use methylated spirits applied to the mealies by means of a swab.

The best thing, though, is to establish a routine, and to treat all your plants at intervals with a systemic insecticide which will keep them free from pests.

The very few less usual members of the lily tribe mentioned here are not to be considered as exclusive. There are other lilies, more spectacular in their way perhaps, which can be grown indoors, and some of these are considered in the sections on flowering plants towards the end of this book. This does not mean, however, that flowering plants are either secondary or second thoughts, but rather that because flowers are, as a general rule, less permanent than foliage, plants noted for them have perhaps less year-round value for their decoration than those which maintain a steady performance at all times.

5. Palms and Other Romantics

There is something about a palm which stirs a sentiment in most of us. How fascinating that these inhabitants of the tropics should have been chosen by us as symbols of leisure, pleasure and relaxation! Palm courts and soft string music; parlour palms and the tinkle of teacups; palm trees and holidays in far-off places – all delightful associations. We tend to overlook the fact that these are trees of vital economic importance in lands where they grow naturally, for they provide the basic materials of life: food, shelter, vessels, rope, even drink.

Palmae is a family consisting of about 1,100 species, only very few of which are grown as pot plants. They are extremely decorative. No other plants provide the same tall, delicately cut silhouette. Although they are true exotics (none is found growing wild in Britain, although a single species, *Chamaerops humilis,* is native to Europe) they are surprisingly easy to cultivate.

The essentials are a well drained soil, plenty of water in the summer, an abundance even, and although watering should be limited in winter their roots should never be allowed to become dry. They need warmth.

A great point in their favour is that they appear to grow best where their roots are restricted, which means that a mature plant can stay in the same pot for several years. As I write I can see a little palm, sold as cocos, which has been growing in a three-inch plastic pot for two years since it was given to me, and possibly for some time before that. Recently I potted it into a four-inch pot, where I hope it will remain for three or four years. This week it has delighted me by producing a little green flower spike. This won't be as magnificent as

48

some blooms, but it is an indication that the plant is doing well and is happy in its surroundings and the treatment it receives.

In the chapter on aechmeas I dealt with the subject of tall plants growing in small pots and the likelihood of them over-balancing and becoming damaged. I said that, fortunately, when we place the little pot in a suitable cover pot the appear-ance of the plant is improved. Palms also benefit by being protected and displayed in the same way. Once again I find that flower arrangement containers, pedestal vases, goblets and similarly shaped vessels display the plants much more effec-tively than a flower-pot-shaped holder.

I also like to plunge the pot, that is, to surround it and have it sitting on some moisture-retentive material. There is then no danger of the pot standing for a long period in a puddle of water and, equally, there is also no danger of the plant's roots drying out. The trouble with pot-bound plants, as these like to be, is that it is difficult to water them pro-perly simply because there is so little soil available to receive, absorb and retain the moisture.

There are many palms to be found on sale. One of my favourites is the dainty *Neanthe bella* from South America. This is a graceful little plant which is slow-growing, a useful if not essential attribute of the house plant. It also has an engaging habit of producing its undistinguished flowers quite freely, and although these are not blooms in the decorative sense, they combine with the foliage to present a pleasing outline.

Palms, too, suffer considerably from synonyms. Neanthe is also known as *Chamaedora elegans* and *C. pulchella,* both names which suggest its grace and beauty. It is the true parlour palm.

The cocos gets its name from the Portuguese for monkey, coco. There is said to be a likeness in the nut to a monkey's head. Botanists, hunting through synonyms for decades, no doubt, have decreed that only the true coconut palm, *C. nucifera,* is a cocos. All the others we used to know under that name now come under other specific titles. I think that all the beginner needs to know is that anything sold under the name of cocos is likely to grow happily and under control at home. He or she is unlikely ever to have a coconut palm pushing up the roof! Little palms like those sold as cocos are very attractive when grown with an assortment of other little slow-growing plants in bottle gardens, where they do very well, growing slowly yet providing height and attractive cover to those below them. They also add variety to the micro-landscape.

It is not such a far cry from coconuts to dates! Often I receive a letter from a reader to say that he or she has successfully germinated a date stone. This is usually followed by a plea for my advice on how to go on from there.

Dates are the fruits of the phoenix palm, *Phoenix dactylifera*. More decorative types of the same genera are known as Stove Feather Palms. The cultivation methods for these apply to most palms. Use a good potting compost, soil or otherwise. My cocos is growing in one of the peat-based or soil-less composts, Kerimure, marketed by I.C.I., and there are others of a similar nature.

Grow the plants in a warm sunny place. Repot or pot seedlings preferably in February or March. Water really abundantly from then on until October. Syringe the foliage morning and evening with clean water from an atomiser from April to September, and after then in the mornings only. Feed with a weak solution of plant food from May to September. Old time gardeners swore by a weak manure water made from cow dung and soot. From March to September the temperature should be roughly between 18-24° C., or 65-75° F. The remainder of the year it will suffice if it is roughly between 13-18° C. or 55-65° F.

If you would like to try your hand at raising date palms, place the stones individually in little pots of properly moistened seed compost. Slip these inside clear plastic bags and fasten them well, so that each bag is as airtight as possible. Place these in an airing cupboard or above a radiator so that the seeds get what gardeners call bottom heat. Germination will vary according to temperature, usually about four to six weeks in a temperature of 21–24° C. and probably some-what longer if it is lower than this. If the compost has been properly moistened and the bag is airtight it should not dry out in this period, but it might be wise to inspect the bags from time to time. I have noticed that when germination begins more condensation appears on the inside of the bag, and after this first appearance it tends to persist. When you see the seed leaf bring the bag into the light, still keeping the little plant snug and warm and moist inside. If it begins to crowd the bag, replace this with a larger one.

There should always be a little condensation on the inside of the bag, especially in the mornings. If this is not apparent there is a strong probability that the compost is not sufficiently moist. If, on the other hand, the condensation appears to you to be excessive, remove the bag, take out the plant, turn the bag inside out, replace the plant and seal the bag again. Repeat this process, if necessary, on other days.

Most nurserymen raise plants from imported seed. However, you can sometimes buy seed quite easily from the best seedsmen. You will probably find listed seeds of *Phoenix roebelinii* and *canariensis,* the dwarf date palm; *Butia capitata* (syn. *Cocos coronata*); *Howea* or *Kentia belmoreana,* the curly palm and *fosteriana,* the flat or thatch leaf palm and *Livingstona chinensis,* the Chinese fan palm.

I am sure that well seasoned professional gardeners will raise their eyebrows to see these plants recommended in a beginner's guide! However, I am prompted to suggest them because I know of so many people who have managed to grow them without the benefits of a special greenhouse.

A little more information on repotting may be helpful. When the seedlings have formed two or three leaves they should be potted into the smallest pots possible that will contain their roots without injury, but only do this if you see that the roots are crowded in their original pots, otherwise wait a little longer. Lift each one carefully avoiding handling the roots. When you place it in its new pot see that no part of the stem is buried; simply keep the soil mark at the old level. For palms this is very important. Rest the base of the leaf part on the soil surface and gently yet firmly ram new soil around the old root ball until the plant feels to be firmly anchored in its new pot. Then test it by gently tugging at a leaf.

Although mature plants grow well with restricted roots young plants should be kept growing and, as gardeners say, moved on when ready. Find the smallest possible pot each time. Never move them from a small pot to one which is much larger. Ramming will be more difficult, but this small move is essential.

Check occasionally to see if the roots are crowding. You can do this by gently turning out the root ball in the same way that a sand pie is turned from a pail. In this case, of course, you need to protect the plant, so slip your first and second fingers along each side of the plant at the point where it rests on the soil, to hold it in place. Upturn the pot and give its rim a sharp tap on another pot or the edge of a table and lift the pot from the root 'pie'. When you have examined this, slip the pot back in place and return the plant to its previous position again, still holding the plant with your fingers in the same way and give the base of the pot a sharp tap to settle the root ball in place again.

When four or five really good leaves have developed the plant can be allowed to settle down in the same pot for a longer period. Thereafter repot only when necessary, choosing the early spring. You will probably find that the roots are very matted and you should take great care not to break them. Although some root damage seems not unduly to affect some plants, certain types of palms will die after such injury.

When the plants are older choose a pot which will allow roughly two inches of space all round, base and sides for the new soil. As I said earlier, I like to use charcoal nuggets for pot drainage. Place these on the base, cover with a little of the new soil and lightly firm it. Set the old root ball on this and then add the new soil little by little all around the roots, ramming it as you go. The palm should be quite happy in this pot for two years at least.

Top dressing can be recommended for palms which have been in the same pot for a considerable time yet do not seem to be in any real need of repotting. This is also a practice from which other types of plants frequently benefit.

First very gently remove the top inch or so of the old soil, scraping it very gently away. Do not dig so deeply that you could injure any roots. Add a little fresh soil until the old level is reached, firming it so that it is much the same consistency as the old.

6. Just Like The Ivy

When one considers the quantity of ivy which grows wild in this country perhaps it will come as a surprise to realise that it is really only recently that we have brought it into our homes and used it as a house plant. No doubt it has suffered from that old alliance of familiarity and contempt!

Hedera helix, or English Ivy as it has been known for a long time in America, where it was a treasured house plant long before the custom became as widespread as it is today, is our common wild ivy. When pot-grown, fed and pampered it takes on a finer and more delicate appearance, but should you return your pot plant to the garden you would gradually notice a change in character. Foliage would thicken in texture and deepen in colour, stems would become more woody and growth more rapid. And by the same token you can pot a piece of wild ivy and grow it indoors where you can watch it gradually take on a more sophisticated refinement.

The ivies form an important and very large section of the house plants available to us. Once again it is a surprise to us when one reads down the long list of varieties to discover that these come from just seven species. However, it seems as though the ivy itself has since tried to make up for this small family in another way – but man has had to help. Instead of new forms appearing as separate plants as has happened in ages past among other genera, the English Ivy, true to the national character, has proved to be an excellent 'sporting' type. All those 'varieties' are really 'sports'.

In gardening terms a sport is a shoot different in character from the typical growth of the plant on which it appears. Imagine it! Someone has a plain green ivy and then one day

54

a new shoot appears, different in colour perhaps, or texture, or size of its leaf from its parent. If this is removed and rooted a new variety is born. I wonder how many ivies have sported unseen?

Often it is the flower which differs rather than the leafy shoot. Roses and chrysanthemums are good examples. Sometimes these will produce a bloom completely different in some way from the others on the same plant.

Those that *H. helix* has produced are fascinating and extraordinarily varied, in colour as well as in the shape and size of the leaves. The leaves of minima, for example, are only a half to one inch across. Many of them well deserve their place in our gardens and you may have seen them clothing a wall or covering an arch in many hues of green, in yellow and green, cream and green and even bronzy purple. And after making a debut in the gardens, now the ivies have come indoors. Thus on a house plant label you are likely to find, say, *H. helix* 'Glacier', and you will know that you are looking at a sport. This, incidentally, is a charming, easy-to-grow plant which has small, neat leaves prettily coloured in grey-green and white. I find it a fine variety for training around a globe of canes or into some other shape.

Helix is also the name for the snail family, and it is given to the ivy as a reference to the way in which the stem twines around a tree trunk. There is not a great deal of twining going on among the ordinary potted ivies and, as a rule, ivies are supported up a cane when you buy them. How you display them is up to you. One in our house has left its cane which reaches from floor to ceiling in the corner by a window in our living room and is now crossing the ceiling to the other corner. Here it clings as it does outside on walls and tree trunks by its adventitious roots. It will, of course, do some superficial damage to the ceiling surface, but no more than is caused by a piece of furniture bumped against a wall, or even the natural dirt that gradually darkens the ceiling surface.

As well as climbing, ivies look well trailing, and one of the prettiest ways to display them is to have them about halfway up a wall facing a window. They will grow quite well away from the light. Here the leaves will gradually all grow to face the window, which means also that they face into the room and you get the best view of them. Each trail will grow so that it gets its full share of light and living space, and this makes for an enchanting and natural mode of growth. Even when climbing, as main stems are helped to go upwards by being tied to a cane, smaller side trails will flow down until a loose column of leaves is formed.

The variations among the ivies means that we can find climbers and trailers for many decorative purposes. A collector will find enough among the helix sports to keep him or her busy for a long time. Some of these will grow quickly and others, such as *H. helix* 'Harald', are slower growing, so obviously the manner in which they are grown and sited will have to depend to some extent on their habit and speed of growth.

The Canary Island Ivy, *H. canariensis,* is a strong climber with large, beautifully coloured leaves which at times are a soft cream. As they mature they are delightfully patterned in grey and dark green. This is a good plant if you wish to soften an arch or doorway in a room, but it will need more light than those with dark green leaves if it is to show at its best.

This plant, in fact, gave me a good object lesson on how light intensity affects growth. It had been planted in an old washstand jug, one with a pattern of violets on it, and stood in a corner of my bedroom some ten feet from the nearest window. And here it remained, almost static, for about three years, developing only two or three new leaves in all that time and not growing noticeably in any way yet showing no sign of sickness. Its leaves had long stems, elongated in fact, and the leaves themselves tended not to be flat but curled and distorted in an unattractive manner.

Then it was transferred into the window itself, and in a few months had grown upwards for two to three feet, producing a pretty stem of flat, nicely marked leaves, each one close to the other. Its treatment had not been changed in any way. The only difference was in the intensity of the light it was receiving.

If large leaves appeal to you there are a number of varieties with this attribute which you will be able to find, although you may have to search a little wider for them since it is generally the small-leaved types which are the most popular.

One word of warning: you may find that an ivy newly brought into your home appears not to be doing very well. Its leaves may be turning brown and falling. This is not always an indication that the plant is dying. Sometimes it is the plant's way of adapting itself to conditions which are strange to it, differing from its previous existence in the comparatively warm, draught-free and humid surroundings of the specialised plant nursery. It may jettison one set of leaves and grow another, apparently more suitable crop. If this should happen you may be advised to spray the stems daily, just lightly, with an atomiser. Once the new leaves have appeared, keep spraying. The indications are that the air in your home is too dry for this particular plant, if not for the others which may by now have accustomed themselves to the drought. It might be wise to install a humidifier for your own sake as well as that of the plants!

All ivies like plenty of water in the summer and little in the winter. I think that it is good to allow the soil to become almost dry before watering again. Soil allowed to remain too wet denies essential oxygen to the plant roots, and soon the leaves will begin to turn yellow and drop. Like the other kinds of plants I have mentioned, they grow best if their pots are plunged.

The plants seem to enjoy much the same temperatures that we do ourselves, and although you might expect that plants which originally have been brought in from our countryside should be quite hardy and able to withstand frosts, this is not so. So many generations of cultivation indoors has left them more tender than they might be thought to be. However, they will stand cool conditions and, as I said earlier, if you plant them out in good weather they will gradually adjust themselves to the different conditions and become good garden plants again.

Much the same applies if you wish to move them around in the house. If they are to go from a warm place to one which is only just above freezing in winter, a porch possibly, move them by degrees if the weather is already cold, or better still wait until summer and allow the plants to acclimatise themselves naturally. Remember, too that the colder the environment the less water the plant will need, generally speaking.

On the whole ivies prefer to be in shade rather than in direct sunlight, but good light conditions usually result in brighter coloured foliage where the plant is variegated. On the other hand, if you are looking for a plant for that no-man's-land under the stairs, in the hall or between the rooms where the windows are either scarce or distant, then the ivy is the one for you.

Plants which are fed, particularly in summer, are much improved in appearance. On our two *H. canariensis,* which we have growing on each side of an archway between rooms, you can see quite clearly the point of growth at which we began to feed them after they were set in place. The leaves are much larger and silkier, and the colours more definite.

You can easily root ivies by placing cuttings in water alone, in soil, in sand, peat or in a good cuttings compost. If it suits you better you can layer them just as easily.

Now I would like, if I may, to introduce you to two of the ivy's relations. One of these is the large-leaved and splendid *Fatsia japonica,* known to many people (incorrectly, as it happens) as the castor oil plant. Its common name should be the false castor oil plant, gained simply because of its considerable resemblance to the annual ricinus, the true castor oil plant. The similarity is in the large palmate leaves rather than anything else. The name fatsia is an adaptation of the Japanese and the specific term *japonica* again tells you that it originated in that country. There is also a splendid and highly decorative variegated form, cream and green.

This is another plant which will grow outdoors as well as in the home. From my window I can see an extremely handsome and very large plant growing on the other side of the lawn. This was one of our house plants until it threatened to take over, so large did it grow even in a comparatively small pot. Obviously, small pots are often more practical, and even then they might be best standing on the floor rather than on a table or in some other raised position. Certainly they are too large for a window sill, although they look attractive on a low table or in a tall window area.

Like the rubber plants they have a contemporary air about them, and are much appreciated by fashionable photographers, who like to site them as they would a piece of sculpture when interiors are being photographed.

Where there is space really large specimens can be grown successfully in pots or tubs, or in some of the many attractive modern vessels in the home. The leaves are softer in texture and their colour is a paler green than when they are grown outdoors, a difference which is quite attractive and not at all detrimental.

A fatsia is really an easy plant to grow. It will need plenty of water in summer, but in winter it will rest and you will need to give it very little, although I think that it helps at this season to keep the leaves well sponged and clean. A weekly bath will make a great deal of difference both to the appearance and to the well-being of the plant. When it is being watered so freely in the summer it will be considerably helped if you feed it freely also. Then its leaves will grow really large and splendidly glossy. It is a plant you can grow in a room without direct sunlight, although obviously it will need some daylight and cannot rely entirely on artificial illumination.

Draughts are fatal, either cold or warm, from door or window or from some form of heater. Those attractive palmate leaves soon flag and the plant looks despondent and unattractive. There is a tremendous difference between the draughts which prevail indoors and the winds that blow outdoors, and where a fatsia will take the second once it has been acclimatised it will never be able to take the first for long periods.

You might one day find flower shoots appearing near the tip of the plant if you have a large and more-or-less mature specimen. Then you will be able to recognise the relationship with the ivy, for the inflorescence of both plants is very similar, and so are the clusters of black berries which follow. You can save these and sow the seed. If you find suckers coming up some distance from the trunk these may also be used for propagation. Move the soil carefully away and pull or cut them away so that a little piece of root remains attached.

There is a good variety of *Fatsia japonica* known as 'Moseri' which was raised in France. It has larger, glossier, more deeply lobed leaves than the type. These have yellow veins. This variety is one of the parents of the second plant I would like to introduce, *Fatshedera lizei*. The other parent is *Hedera helix hibernica,* the so-called Irish ivy. There are two forms of this plant. One has deep green leaves and the other is flecked and margined with cream and known as variegata.

It is most unusual to find a hybrid of two separate and different genera like this.

The fatshedera, as the name suggests, retains some of the characteristics of each type: the palmate leaves of the fatsia and the sprawling or creeping habit of the ivy when it grows on the ground. It will not cling as the ivy does. In commerce the plants are always trained to grow upright, their stems being tied to a cane. I once saw a plant in a garden which had been allowed to sprawl. It was a large one and it looked most attractive displayed this way, although this would not be practical in the average home.

This is not a plant which looks well growing isolated. As it ages the base of its stem becomes bare. Its tip can be pinched out if it grows too tall. It is a good component in a mixture of plants where it can tower above the others. It is easy and tolerant.

It likes best to be kept just moist around the roots and grown in the semi-shade. However, I have found that it will tolerate most conditions. If it is fed in the summer months it will make good and often rapid growth.

Plants plunged into moist peat in a larger cover pot, like this saintpaulia, receive many benefits – not least of which is the constant humidity created round the leaves as the moisture evaporates from below

One of the easiest of all house plants, *Aechmea rhodocyanea*, a bromeliad, can be watered simply by filling the 'vase' made by its cupped leaves. Its long-lasting flower is vividly coloured

Ficus vary considerably within the family. This dainty, tree-like, *F. benjamina* differs greatly in appearance from the large-leaved, single stemmed rubber plant, but it is a little less house-hardy

Air-layering, a convenient form of propagation, applied to a variegated form of Ficus Decora which has grown too tall. When roots form and grow into the moss under the plastic, the tip is detached and potted as a new plant

Grown for its chunky handsome and long-lived foliage, the sansevieria sometimes flowers. Although the spikes of creamy blooms are not highly decorative they are extremely fragrant, like many lilies to which they are closely related

Chlorophytum capense sends out long stolons on each of which grow tiny, starry lily-like flowers followed by a terminal plantlet. This plant shares a bowl with rhoeo, helxine and *Begonia rex*

Phoenix dactylifera, the date palm, one of the many house hardy and highly decorative 'parlour' palms. Like most of its tribe, when out of the seedling stage, it grows best when its roots are restricted in a small pot

Hedera or ivy has few species but many varieties. Those in this group show the diversity of leaf shape and size, as well as the colour variegations which can be found. The greener the leaves the less light the plants will tolerate

One of the easiest to grow of all trailers, *Plectranthus fruticosus*, a labiate plant nearly related to the more vividly coloured coleus. Cuttings of both plants root easily, and will continue to grow in pebbles and water without soil

Philodendrons are varied in form and habit. Their shining green foliage is always decorative. *P. bipinnatifidum* with *P. Imbe*, which has handsome, burgundy-red shoots and stems, in the foreground

All climbers do better if they are encouraged to climb. Usually they are supported by canes or string. Here, on Rochford's nursery, a monstera has been encouraged to root into a moist plank of wood as though it were a tree

Rhoicissus, one of the members of the grape vine family, makes a most agreeable house plant. A young plant such as this will grow several feet in a year and can be prettily trained round a door or window

Also of the grape family, *Cissus antarctica*, as its specific name suggests, prefers a cool atmosphere so long as it is frost free. It is the ideal plant for a sunless room but it needs good daylight

One of the most popular of all house plants, the little tradescantia colours best where the light is most intense. A trailer or scrambler by habit, it can be kept controlled by pinching out the tips of the stems, which make good cuttings and will root easily either in water or in a cuttings compost. Carefully snip off the leaves from the lower portion of stem and insert this into the rooting medium

A gorgeous plant from my neighbour's windowsill, a leaf-flowering cactus or epiphyllum. It can produce dozens of lovely blooms along the edges of its 'leaves' – which really are its stems

Good companions! Succulent agave and aloe share a bowl with a cactus. The flower spike of the former is to the left of the cactus flowers. The striped aloe is also known as the partridge plant

One of the many handsome and extremely distinctive members of the crassula family – an echeveria in bloom. Although often small, the blooms are very beautiful both in form and colour

A neighbour's, *Aeonium tabulaeforme*, of the crassula family. It sends up handsome spikes of pale yellow flowers from the centres of the rosettes, which themselves are like great green roses

Bulbs can be grown without soil in several ways. The polyanthus narcissus here, Cragford, grows best in pebbles and water. The pink hyacinths are in bulb fibre

7. Plectranthus and Puddle Pots

How pleasant for me to be able to say of a plant that it is one of the easiest of all to grow indoors. This is so true of the pretty trailing plectranthus. My first aquaintance was with *P. fruticosus,* which has glossy, lobed, almost heart-shaped leaves.

I saw it at a friend's house and it was the way it grew which appealed to me. It filled the corner of a long shelf which stretched along the width of the wall which faced a great window. In the corner two smooth wooden poles reached from shelf to ceiling. The plectranthus was supported by these and grew upwards gracefully. But more than that, it covered a large area of the shelf itself, filling the corner with a mass of foliage and then cascading over the shelf edge. Each leaf turned towards the light. The tip of every trail turned upwards in a gentle curve, giving the entire, dense, leafy mass a dainty and graceful appearance. My first plant was a cutting from this one.

It is the easiest thing in the world to take cuttings, stem cuttings. There are other kinds such as leaf and root cuttings. All you have to do is to nip off the growing tip, some three to four inches long, at the end of one of the many stems. Remove the lowest leaves so that you are left with enough bare stem to insert in soil, cutting compost or even water. In a few days the roots begin to grow from the stem and a new plant is formed.

Once there are plenty of roots on cuttings struck in water the plant can be potted up in the normal manner. One friend of mine compromises this way. Once there are good roots he begins adding a little compost or soil to the water so that it is first of all a form of mud. When more is added it gradually becomes moist soil. Meanwhile the roots grow into the soil. When the little pot is full the plant is repotted into a slightly larger pot in the usual way.

c

When you take a stem cutting from any plant cut the shoot just below a joint or node, to use the botanical term. Be careful not to tear the leaves off or you may strip the skin from the stem. These are best cut with scissors or a sharp knife. The reason for this is that there is always a bud in the axil between leaf and stem, the point where one joins the other. It is the tiny buds on the portion inserted in the soil or water which grow into roots, and so these must be protected.

My *Plectranthus fruticosus* grew apace, but I never saw another on sale! This species seems to be distributed only by one friend passing on a cutting to another. However, now an even more decorative species, *P. oertendahlii*, is often to be seen on sale in nurseries and garden centres. I have plants of this also. It really is a charming plant and trails as attractively as the first one I saw. Its colouring is more distinctive.

Its description in that fabulous (and so heavy!) *Exotica,* a 2,000-page American encyclopaedia of plants, pleases me: ". . . fleshy creeper with four angled stem and small broad leaves, friendly green to bronzy, patterned with an attractive network of silvery veins". I like the "friendly green". Perhaps because of my name I have a liking for violet, purple and similar hues, tints and shades, and this is one reason why I find this plectranthus so pleasing. The undersides of its leaves are purple and this becomes a deeper, richer violet under certain conditions. The plant I have which grows in the bowl along with the ivy and asparagus is an example.

P. oertendahlii originated in Natal. It has given us a really beautiful sport, *P.o. variegatus,* which has small, fleshy, almost chunky leaves coloured and margined with white. So far I have not seen a great many isolated plants on sale. Florists like it and use it in those handsome gift bowls they assemble for the Christmas trade. If you receive one of these be sure to take a cutting right away.

Plectranthus are one of a group of plants known as labiates. This means that they have lipped flowers. Salvias and many other herbs are good examples. Actually the little flowers of the various plectranthus are not the most decorative features of the plants and when they do appear it is better for the well-being of the plant that they should be nipped off. The plant then goes back to the business of producing the pretty leaves and those attractive trails.

Plectranthus will grow in the sunlight, but it really does best in shade, or if this is not convenient or practical, in a north window rather than a sunny one. It does not grow in dry, centrally heated rooms unless the pot can be plunged in the way I have already described. Dry heat is bad for it.

One other trailing labiate is often to be seen growing in containers, more usually in hanging baskets, but I feel that I should mention it here because it is also a tenant of a cottage window where is hangs prettily in sun or shade. This is the ground ivy, *glecoma,* which you may see growing wild in hedgerows.

In the wild it spreads over the ground, sometimes climbing up through the plants which surround it, but when it is pot-grown it is allowed to trail. The long stems of lobed, kidney-shaped leaves are studded with violet-coloured flowers in spring and early summer.

The plain green leaved species *G. hederacea* (synonyms are *Nepeta glechoma* and *N. hederacea*) is not often seen. Instead the variegated form is more popular. It is very easy to grow.

Now let us leave the trailers for a moment and discuss some closely related plants which grow in a different manner, the beautifully coloured coleus and in particular varieties of *Coleus blumei,* some of which are so gorgeously coloured that they have been given special varietal names.

I grow masses of plants each year, not named varieties but mixtures raised from a packet of seeds sown each spring. I sow these thinly in wide pans or even in bulb bowls, whatever happens to be convenient at the time. Each vessel is given a layer of charcoal as drainage and I use one of the many good peat-based seed composts. This is first made moist enough so that when a handful is squeezed lightly it holds together. It must never be so wet that water drips out when it is squeezed. The bowls are filled to within about an inch from the rim.

The very fine seed is sown on the surface and very lightly covered. The container is then slipped inside a clear plastic bag. This is sealed tightly at the mouth so the bag is made as airtight as possible. It is then placed in the airing cupboard. Failing this, it can be stood on a warm window sill or near a radiator, anywhere, in fact, where the temperature will be about 24°C.

A close watch is kept, for as soon as the seeds germinate they must be brought into good light. Once they develop too far in the dark and become drawn they will not mature well. Mine spend their early days on a window sill and are kept inside the bag until the little seedlings are large enough to handle.

From this point they must be pricked off into a potting compost and, if you wish, into individual pots. However, I don't grow them this way. I have discovered a more interesting, and certainly more decorative method. If you havn't a greenhouse dozens of tiny pots about the place can be a nuisance rather than a pleasure, so I plant several seedlings together into one container.

For this I use a great many different vessels, from bulb bowls to flower vases of suitable shape. I never plant fewer than seven together, and often I plant many more, depending upon the size of the container. All are about three inches apart every way.

This has proved to be an attractive and delightful way of growing these plants. Each summer we have great bowls of gorgeous colour about the house and I always have enough to pass some on as gifts. Each plant varies so much from the others in hue and pattern that several make a wonderful colour harmony, and they seem to mind not at all that they are not in true flower pots.

Incidentally, it seems to me, after observing them for so many years now, that they do better in shallow bowls than in deep ones. At the moment quite the prettiest and strongest display is in a bowl no more than two inches deep.

If among the many plants you get from one packet of seed you find one or more which appeals to you, you can, as I described earlier with the plectranthus, propagate them from cuttings at any time of the year. They usually root very quickly. The cuttings are usually inserted in individual pots, kept moist and shaded from the sun and grown on in a temperature of not less than about 10–12°C.

Once the are more or less mature coleus begin to flower and

here it is possible to see their resemblance to the plectranthus. Once again the flowers are not really highly decorative and, just as with the plectranthus, the plant improves if these are kept nipped off. This induces the stems to produce more foliage. In the same way it helps when plants are young if you pinch the tips from them to induce them to grow bushy and well shaped rather than tall and perhaps somewhat straggly.

Both coleus and plectranthus need to be watered freely in summer and only moderately in winter. Actually it is probably best to throw out old plants of coleus once they begin to look leggy and shabby, and begin again with new. Cuttings taken in September will produce good plants.

As you would expect, since they have such good, strong colours and are so variegated, coleus need plenty of light. They also need some warmth.

Apart from the fact that I like the look of them, I also grow both plectranthus and coleus because they are so good for including in what I have named puddle pots. In these the plants grow in water and not in soil. Their roots are anchored by pebbles. They are nourished by soluble plant food applied at intervals, and the water level is, of course, kept topped up.

The plants can be all of one kind or mixed. I think that a mixture looks best. They can be held in any kind of water-tight container you fancy so long as it is deep enough to hold a good layer of pebbles or small stones – shingle for example. I have used lidless gravy tureens, teapots, flower vases, soup bowls and several others.

Since I introduced puddle pots many readers have written to me to describe their successes, and I believe that this really is an ideal form of indoor gardening for the true beginner.

The coleus gives a bright splash of colour to the other plants used, and the plectranthus is delightful in the way it trails over the rims of the containers to give the new little garden an established and mature appearance.

You do not have to start off with fully grown plants. Instead you can merely arrange a variety of cuttings and leave them to root and go on growing. If you use rooted plants wash the roots carefully before arrangement.

If you paid regard to my earlier remarks, that good soil was essential to good growth, you will appreciate that plants grown in puddle pots will never make the lush growth that they would in soil. Leaves are smaller, growth slower, but this results in a light and dainty appearance. Of the plants I have mentioned so far in this book, chlorophytum and ivies are suitable for this form of gardening with, of course, the subjects of this chapter, plectranthus and coleus. You can also grow philodendrons, rhoicissus, tradescantia and others, all of which will be discussed in following chapters.

To make the puddle pot have all your cuttings or plants (or a mixture of both) ready beside you. You will need charcoal nuggets to strew on the floor of the container to keep the water sweet and enough pebbles to hold the plants securely in position. If you first place a shallow layer of sand on the floor of the container you can easily embed charcoal and the first layer of stones in it.

I would recommend this if you are using a highly glazed container, because the first pebbles tend to slip about somewhat, which is a little disconcerting. Get a good layer of pebbles in place and then begin to arrange the plants. Think about this and place trailers so that they can flow over the rim, and position neat, compact plants like chlorophytum, or gaily coloured kinds like the coleus at the centre, where they can make a pretty focal point and tie the rest together. As each plant or cutting is set in place anchor it with a stone or two until all are safely settled.

The stems should be supported by the pebbles up to rim level. If you wish, you can arrange some prettier stones or even sea shells on the surface. However, once the puddle pot's contents get growing well you will find that the surface is hidden, so this is not very important except at the very early stages. Pour in the water, but keep this just below rim level.

If the trailers grow too long for your liking, keep them nipped back. You can use the pieces you remove to start other puddle pots.

Don't be in a hurry to feed the cuttings. Wait until the roots are growing well. Be sure, meanwhile, to keep the water level topped up, even more important than when the plants grow in soil. The plants will need feeding about once a month. Give a very weak solution at first and then gradually increase it, but never overdo it. It is always better to give too little plant food than too much.

8. Tree Lovers or Philodendrons

If you have ever searched the country hedgerows in spring looking for the green, leafy lords and ladies or cuckoo pint, then you are already acquainted with our native representative of one member of the family to be discussed in this chapter, the Araceae. You may also know other arum 'lilies', the snowy white, purple and bright yellow zantedeschias, also sometimes called calla lilies. Actually none is a lily but an aroid. There are many aroids which are excellent house plants. The showy and sculpturally beautiful climber, *Monstera deliciosa,* is one of their race. Known popularly as the Swiss Cheese Plant because the leaves have dramatic holes and indentations, the monstera is usually seen as a shrub, but it will grow to 50 feet or more in length, given good support.

If you have one of these plants long enough and grow it well enough for it to bloom you will see the family likeness in the strange green flowers. These are followed by a long, pitted, cone-shaped and delicious fruit, the bread-fruit, savouring of a blend of bananas and pineapple here, which gives the plant its specific name when it answers to monstera. Its synonym *Philodendron pertusam* means that the leaves are perforated with round or oblong holes.

So far as our house plants are concerned, the araceae is one of the most important families. We call all the members aroids. There are altogether more than 1,000 species in 105 genera, and most of them come from the tropics. Many are jungle plants, and as one would expect their origins affect the way we should care for them. They vary considerably in habit, which means that we can find plants suited to a variety of decorative uses. You can grow many as simple pot plants, arums, zantedeschias, callas, spathiphyllums, anthuriums and others, and these all have

68

handsome flowers. So far as the climbers are concerned their blooms are not of great consequence because of the way that we have to grow them, yet they are so ornamental that they form one of the largest and most popular groups of house plants, not only in Britain, but all over the world.

These climbers are extremely interesting. They are epiphytes. Indeed, the name of the most popular kind, the philodendrons, comes from *phileo*, to love, and *dendron*, a tree. They have two kinds of roots, one kind with which they climb by clinging to their support. These may not be much in evidence in plants grown in a house. The other kind, known as aerial roots, hang dangling from the main stem, even in our homes, searching for the precious and essential moisture which they convey to their leaves.

Aerial roots which appear on our house plants are best trained down into the soil in the pot if this is possible, although frequently they are produced too high in the air for this to be done.

As you would expect, some aroids are easier to grow than others. Not all are plants for the beginner, for some like a warm, moist atmosphere difficult to reproduce or simulate in the home. However, there are many which are easy, tough and adaptable, which is as one would expect from so popular, well known and wide ranging a family.

The easiest of the climbers in my opinion is the one which has been around the longest, *Philodendron scandens*. It is a neat plant with dark green, heart-shaped leaves and slim stems which, although they climb well in nature, usually need to be supported when the plant is pot-grown. On the other hand, these also trail prettily. It is a friendly plant, growing well in light or shade. It doesn't even sulk if it is over-watered, although it cannot tolerate this for long periods. It will even grow entirely in water, as, for example, when planted in a puddle pot.

If you wish to grow it really well, remember that it is an epiphyte and make a tree for it to love. You can do this by covering a support, perhaps a forked branch or maybe only a wooden stake, with moss, sphagnum type for preference. Tie it on and keep it sprayed so that it continues to grow and remains nicely moist and inviting to the philodendron's roots, which will gradually grow into it. I have seen these roots, in fact, even grow into a plank of wood which was kept moist!

Another method you can use instead of the sometimes diffi-cult and messy moss is to cut a block of Oasis (used normally for flower arrangement) into equal sections each wide enough to allow a cane to be passed through their centres thus linking each block together until the cane is covered. Leave a clear end portion to be inserted down into the pot. Alternatively, thread the ready-shaped cylinders of Oasis onto a cane. Keep the plastic moist and the roots will grow into it in just the same way that they will grow into moss. Plants grown this way will become lush and leafy. If, however, you wish to keep your plant looking very much as it did when you first acquired it, the thing to do is to keep it a little on the dry side in its orginal pot and not to feed it.

There are a great many philodendrons, both species and varieties, in cultivation but there are not a great number easily to be found on sale. Some are really tenants for the warm green-house, but others are just not an economic proposition for the large-scale plant producers, and so are neglected except for the smaller specialists, from whom you can still obtain them if you care to search hard and long enough.

One of my favourites, a tried and true friend, is *Philodendron imbe,* sometimes sold under the popular name of Burgundy. Actually imbe is a Brazilian Indian name for most climbing plants of this race, but it happens to have become the specific name for a species which is slow to climb and which has long, arrow-shaped leaves. There are many handsome cultivars of the species. Mine is now many years old. Its young leaves, which grow from a tight sheath on the stem, are a beautiful red-purple. The old ones, which incidentally are very long lived, are a deep green with a purple-copper sheen and dark, wine-red under-sides.

Parenthetically, this might be a good place to say that, where-as in the garden we like our plants to grow quickly, to grow large and to grow handsome, these are not characteristics or habits we look for in our house plants, otherwise they would soon outgrow their space. Instead, the best house plants are those which remain looking always young and decorative, yet which grow so slowly that they can occupy their allocated position for years at a time, much the same as a picture or a piece of furniture will do.

My *Philodendron imbe* is watered once a week, but it is plunged inside a tall outer pot of peat so that conditions around its roots are always moist though never sodden. A little more water is required by imbe than by most philodendrons. In winter water should be applied with care, for it needs only enough to prevent its roots from drying out, a matter which is usually seen to by the moist peat surrounding the pot.

Another old and revered member of our family is *Philodendron bipinnatifidum,* which means that it has feathered leaves. This is not a climber, and in nature it grows as a stout tree. In my house it stands on a pedestal in a space between two bookshelves, some eight feet or so from the nearest windows. The great light green leaves grow up from the centre in the manner of a tree fern, and the lower ones flow down over the pot rim. The whole unit has a graceful and extremely attractive appearance. This plant also is plunged, and it is from this source that its only humidity comes, because the leaves cannot normally be sprayed without harming the furnishings nearby. Yet in spite of the fact that it is said to need both warmth and great humidity it has grown there for many years, gradually increasing the number of its leaves and its overall size.

Architecturally the monstera is as important a part of the contemporary decorative scene as the rubber plant. It needs the right setting to display itself properly. Ours finally outgrew the studio where my husband and I work. It was obvious that it would have climbed many more feet if only we could have allowed it to have its head. But it had to go and we miss its dramatic presence. And we still have rather wary memories of the one we grew in our London studio, which grew twelve feet to the ceiling and then ten feet along before we decided that enough was enough, and of the specimen we saw growing happily in a Belgian dockside estaminet, fully 30 feet long!

The deep green leaves are so punctured and patterned with holes that some people call it the Gruyere cheese plant, which seems to me undignified for such a handsome aroid.

This plant boasts two names, monstera when it is adult and *Philodendron pertusum* when it is young. Like our own native ivy, the young of some of these climbers do not always resemble their adult forms and can easily be mistaken for an entirely different species. If you can, inspect the shape of the leaves on the branch of adult, berried ivy and see how these differ from the characteristic pointed foliage on a climbing trail growing close to a wall or a tree trunk. Once the ivy reaches both a certain height and a certain maturity it changes its character, becomes more shrub-like and alters the shape of its leaves. The same applies to certain tropical climbers, and there are, of course, certain perfectly logical genetic reasons for this change.

There are altogether about 30 species of monstera. There is also a pretty, variegated form of deliciosa. This is not quite so house-hardy as the green form, which is, in fact, the most adaptable of them all, and so makes an excellent plant for the beginner.

The monstera likes a shady position, and once having been placed in the home it should be left alone. Every time I have had to move a monstera because it has finally outgrown its situation it has thereafter failed to thrive, even though there seemed to be little difference in the environment so far as one could see. The plant sulks and refuses to produce another leaf. It says there static, until the original leaves become old and stale and brown and the plant has to be thrown out.

Unlike the other plants I have discussed so far it likes plenty of root room and a really large pot, another reason why this is really a plant for large interiors. It will grow well and for years in a smaller container, but only when the roots have space to roam will the leaves achieve their characteristic slashed and holed appearance. In a smaller pot they tend to remain small and solid.

It also needs plenty of water in all but the deepest and darkest of winter, when the soil should be kept only just moist. It should be fed occasionally. Its great beautiful leaves should be groomed to remove dust and also occasionally sprayed when possible with clean water.

It can be propagated by air layering, a good way to reduce a plant which has grown too large.

One could write a book on aroid house plants alone, but not all of them are suitable for the beginner and so many of my favourites will not be mentioned here. However, I would like to introduce one of those agreeable house plants which will tolerate the unskilled administrations of the novice, the goose foot plant, or *Syngonium podophyllum.* The shape of the leaf gives it its folk name. Botanically, podophyllum means merely that the leaves are stalked.

There are about fourteen species and many varieties in cultivation, although few are commercially available. Some of them are prettily marked, often with the veins delineated by white lines. Others are most highly or dramatically variegated.

Although I said that it was a good natured plant I hasten to add that a plant which is poorly treated is nothing like as handsome as one which has had careful and considerate handling. It likes a warm and draught-free environment, light shade and plenty of water in summer. The soil must be kept drier in winter. Cuttings can be used in puddle pots.

9. Vines without Grapes

Earlier in this book I remarked on the confusion which can be caused by the use of common names, and it looks sometimes as though even the botanists were once at fault, or at least could put us at fault sometimes. Take the cissus, for example, a genus of about 200 species belonging to the grape family, Vitaceae. No one called them Vitus or anything similar as one might expect. Instead they receive their name from the Greek word Kissos, which means ivy! This has nothing at all to do with the plant, but instead was an allusion to the way the plants climb. So here we are with an ivy which is really a grape and is called a cissus!

Many cissus plants are most likely to be found in greenhouses or conservatories, where they make handsome and effective roof climbers. The one most often grown in the home is *Cissus antarctica,* the kangaroo vine, so named because it comes from Australia.

This is a useful climber which seems to live forever once it finds an environment to its liking. It dislikes direct sunlight, and any failures I have had with it have been when the plant stood in too sunny a place. As its name suggests, it will withstand cold to a certain degree. It hates draughts, especially hot, dry currents of air, and these are likely to affect the growing tips, causing them to shrivel and young leaves to drop.

Once it has settled in it grows apace like a vine, and one must keep up with it, tying in the new shoots to canes or strings as they lengthen. It is just the plant for filling in the corner of a room. It does not seem noticeably to recognise the difference in the seasons as much as some plants. Because of this it is as well to keep it going with moderate feeding throughout the year.

Although you can buy quite large plants (and incidentally these can be ideal if you wish to instal some kind of instant decoration for a special occasion) generally speaking I think that it is best for the beginner to start with a small plant. This is much more likely to settle down quickly and grow into its surroundings by way of making itself at home.

Another plant, known to some as grape ivy, is sometimes also called *Cissus rhombifolia,* but it is more widely and correctly known as *Rhoicissus rhomboidea.* I find this the easiest climber in existence. It too will live for years and will cover an entire wall if carefully trained and supported. Training involves directing new trails in the required direction and is simplicity itself. These trails will soon take hold of any support provided by their tendrils. My own plants are first tied to a cane, which as a rule stretches from pot to ceiling. From this I fasten either fine string or stout thread to support the trails which have reached the top of the cane and wish now to move hoirzontally. Once the trails grow really well they hide the supports, which then become quite invisible.

I find this rhoicissus so adaptable. The largest plants in my home have been raised by layering. I chose this method of propagation because in each case I wanted the plants to grow in containers which were not well suited for the usual methods of planting. One plant grows in a large willow-pattern china jug, once part of a washstand set. This stands on the floor in one corner of a room. The plant quite fills the corner, and indeed low growing trails now hide the jug too. The climbing trails are now on their way along the top of the wall in each direction.

The other plant grows in a gallon pickle jar which has a very narrow neck. There it has been growing steadily for many years since it was first layered from a large plant, which has been parent to a great number of daughters now scattered about the country.

Yet another grows in a fairly shallow wash basin, and this plant has a rather remarkable history. It was planted in the basin in the first place to see just what would happen to it, for this was in the days when the pundits were saying that plants would never grow in glazed containers without drainage holes. It was already tall and about five years old when we decided to make improvements to our cottage. Unfortunately, as the builders moved in we had to move out several large plants, but I refused to give away this particular rhoicissus. Instead it was temporarily housed in an unheated caravan. As it was so tall it had to be propped up on its side at a slant and it stretched almost the entire length of its shelter. There it remained for many months. During the coldest weather the soil was kept almost, but not quite, bone dry. "It will never survive," I was told. But it did, and it now stands in a new room attractively growing around an archway and still sending out new trails, while it remains clothed with foliage right the way down to bowl level.

The important thing for the beginner to grasp is that this plant, now several feet in length, still grows in its original soil. There is little room in the bowl that is not occupied by roots, enough space near the rim to facilitate watering. This means that we cannot top dress with new soil and as the roots are so near the surface neither can we scrape some of the spent soil away and replace it with new. So the soil remaining is kept fertile with soluble plant food administered once a week when the plant is watered. As you can imagine, by watering time the soil is dry and because of this it is well aerated as the fresh water rushes down and fills the drainage area at the base of the container.

Not all plants would grow well under such conditions, but many climbers will, and indeed will flourish so long as they are kept fed and propery watered.

At the same time climbers will also grow very slowly and you can control the speed of growth to a certain degree by with-holding both food and water. The rhoicissus, for instance, is a good plant for a puddle pot. The most it will do when mixed with other plants is make one good and attractive trail. This can be shortened if and when this is necessary, and it will then become more bushy.

There are other cissus, but most of the others need such a high degree of humidity that they are not really suitable for the average home. However, if you feel that you are successful in growing pot plants and would like to try your hand at something a little more demanding, look for *Cissus striata,* sometimes called the miniature grape ivy. This is a dainty, prettily marked plant with five-part leaves and fine tendrils.

10. Happy Wanderers

One of the most frequently seen of our house plants, growing almost everywhere that an indoor plant is to be seen, the happy wanderer carries a little piece of history in its botanical name, for it remembers John Tradescant, gardener to Charles I. It was brought from the new world, which with its treasures animal, vegetable and mineral, was at that time becoming increasingly revealed to the west. And surely many of the exotic plants which survived the long journey over the perilous seas must have seemed every bit as wonderful as those other treasures. They differed from them, too, for plants can eventually be shared by all. But at first, as we see, they were treasured jealously and maintained under royal patronage.

There are about 100 species of the genus Tradescantia in the family Commelinaceae, all of them herbaceous, no shrubs at all. The habit and foliage are extremely variable. Those who grow *Tradescantia virginiana,* the common spiderwort, in their gardens can hardly be expected instantly to recognise the relationship between this erect, untidy, long-leaved plant with its umbels of inch-wide flowers and the dainty, trailing pot plant with its variegated foliage which decorates not only homes but thousands of offices and school rooms up and down the country.

Although the individual flowers of the garden types last only a day, the plant itself is well worth a place in any flower border because the short lived blooms follow each other in quick succession. The pot plant species, on the other hand, are grown chiefly for the beauty of their leaves. Mature plants will flower but the blooms, though quite pretty in their quiet way, are really undistinguished. On the other hand the leaves can be as bright as any flower if the plant is grown well.

Most often seen is *Tradescantia fluminensis,* also called wandering Jew and wandering sailor, a 'trivial' name which gives us an indication of the manner in which it grows. This plant is greatly affected by light intensity. Where the light is good the leaves become beautifully coloured. The undersides and the tips of the stems are in amethyst hues and the striped upper surfaces shine with an underlying frosty glitter which is very attractive. However, if the plant grows way back in some dim corner of a room the leaves may be a dull green, unremarkable and unattractive, and if the trails are allowed to grow too long they may present the appearance of singed string.

Although one would think that the species, *T. fluminensis,* or the Rio tradescantia as it is sometimes called, was in itself sufficiently coloured, it has produced a variegated form whose leaves are a fresh apple-green striped with clear bands of yellow and cream.

The popularity of the tradescantia tribe demonstrates that it is easily grown. When plants are first bought they are usually neat and compact, the stems short and even upright. But as the species is a trailer the shoots soon elongate. If it is kept well fed these trails grow vigorously and are extremely handsome. Properly situated such plants can be highly decorative. But if they are not cared for they can become straggly, with many brown and faded leaves giving the entire plant a shabby and unkempt appearance.

In this case the stems should be cut right back, even almost to pot rim. The plant should then be fed and regularly watered and before long it will produce new and healthier growth. If you prefer a compact, not too trailing type of plant, then the thing to do is to keep nipping out the tops of the stems when these have grown to just beyond the length required. The plant will come to no harm and will probably even be improved.

If you like to produce new plants, the shoots which are cut away can be used as cuttings. These will root quickly in moist compost, sand, or even in plain water. Tradescantia and company are ideal for puddle pots.

Tradescantias grow best if they are given plenty of water during the summer but rather less in winter, although this will depend to a great extent on the temperature of the room in which they stand and the quantity and quality of light they receive. They thrive in a warm atmosphere, but here as usual one must ensure that there is some humidity available to the plant. Fortunately it is quite possible to plunge the pots, even if these are placed on a wall or a high shelf.

Incidentally, one must always watch for hot, dry draughts when any plants are placed more than five or six feet from the ground. Warm air rises and often, without you being aware of it, a plant can be in an atmosphere which will soon kill it. If such an elevated place is the only one available, do see that the plunge pot is continually inspected and that the peat or whatever else is used is kept constantly moist. If it is possible to spray the leaves then this will help. One of the loveliest tradescantias I have seen, a golden variety, was growing in the window of a friend's bathroom. There was no gas water heater, just a beautifully clean atmosphere which became ideally humid at certain times each day. The plant trailed from the window sill almost to the ground, each trail fully furnished with colourful leaves.

Chunkier in appearance than *T. fluminensis* is *T. blossfeldiana,* a handsome plant which also produces umbels of pretty little flowers, each some half inch across. These are bicoloured, pink on the upper half and white on the lower. However, this is not quite such an easy plant for the beginner because it needs both warmth and a good degree of humidity. But if you find that the other tradescantias grow well with you, then perhaps you would like to try this one.

First, though, try another species, zebrina, whose name is a reference to the zebra-like stripes on the leaves. These also have the beautiful 'frosty' sheen which in some lights gives the plants an almost metallic appearance. This sheen is evidence of a well grown plant, so you can congratulate yourself if your plant sparkles.

Zebrina pendula is often confused with tradescantia yet the differences are really quite recognisable. The first plant is considerably larger than the other and generally of a more fleshy appearance. The leaves are differently coloured. These are striped with a silvery grey-green and mauve. The undersides are a richer mauve, often a fine purple. Although it, too, is a trailer it grows more slowly.

There are several varieties. The markings on Z. *pendula discolor* are not so definite as in pendula but even so they are quite lovely, the main colour of the leaf being a purple-copper with two narrow silver bands running down the leaf. My favourite is Z.*p.d. multicolor,* which has large ovate leaves with stripes and bands of creamy pink in addition to the other hues. Other varieties of zebrina are a little delicate, and in any case may be difficult for the layman to obtain.

These plants are all adaptable, and besides being both easy to grow and attractive on their own are ideal tenants in mixed arrangements. As you would expect, they look well planted near the rim of any container, where they can trail prettily over the edge.

It is important, I think, that when they are to be used this way the height of the container be taken into consideration, because a strong trailer growing over the edge of a low bowl soon looks out of place. It can become a nuisance too, getting very much in the way, and it is likely to become damaged when the plant is moved. It is best to elevate the plant in some way so that the trails can hang more or less unimpeded.

Besides looking well in tall and pedestal containers or displayed in wall brackets and on shelves, tradescantia and zebrina both look attractive in hanging baskets. These are just the things for growing in a sunny window and they need not be large. It is possible to manufacture a conveniently sized 'basket' from a plastic bowl or colander, as well as from wire netting. These plants may also be used out of doors in summer in mixtures of plants in traditional hanging baskets containing mainly the popular types of bedding plants.

There are other decorative and interesting plants in this genus although these may not be for the absolute beginner. However, they are worth keeping in mind for those gardeners who hope to extend their scope. They include the handsome

Rhoeo discolor or spathacea, which has a stiff rosette of waxy, metallic leaves, green above and purple underneath, which at first sight resembles a bromeliad; *Setcreasea purpurea* or purple heart, so named because of the vivid hue the plant assumes in strong sunlight and *Commelina benghalensis*. The last is fairly delicate, needing a warm temperature and some humidity, but its little flowers which last only for a day are as rare and beautiful a blue as any you will find.

11. The Prickly Subject of Cacti

It always pleases me to write about cacti because like the bromeliads these are among the few plants for which I can give more or less explicit instructions about watering and feeding.

Cacti, however, seem to be an acquired taste, for while there are many people who find them absolutely fascinating and beautiful there are others who declare that they hate them. It seems that there are few who merely tolerate these strange growths.

For they *are* strange! Especially when we compare them with more familiar plants. In the first place they rarely have leaves, a disconcerting fact for those who like to grow a plant for the sake of its foliage alone. Instead of leaves most have a thick, succulent stem known as the plant body. Sometimes this branches, but even then not in the familiar, old and comforting manner of a tree or even a herbaceous plant.

Cacti have become adapted to the environment in which they grow, and in their native state the great thing to their advantage is that they are able to retain moisture even under conditions of excessive drought. When you consider how successful some have become at living in desert conditions it is not really surprising that some other plants have become adapted in a similar manner. These much resemble cacti in appearance and this resemblance can cause considerable confusion, especially to the new gardener.

To put it simply, we say that a cactus is succulent if we wish to describe its appearance in everyday language. At the same time, botanically, it is 'a succulent' because this is the term given to all thick and fleshy plants. In those other than cacti, stems or leaves or quite often both may be thick and fleshy. We have already met some of them from the lily family, aloe and sansevieria for example.

A simple thing to bear in mind is that although all cacti are succulents, not all succulents are cacti. Once you get to know cacti well you are not likely to confuse one with another. Unfortunately cacti and other succulent plants are often marketed together in the same box and are sold under the omnibus and incorrect name of cacti, which adds to the confusion. Often one finds them planted together in the same bowl, and broadly speaking there is no reason culturally, why they should not be.

Not only the lily family produces succulent members. Most other plant families have one or more succulent species. You probably know one in the daisy family quite well. This is the mesembryanthemum, that gorgeous and colourful seaside plant which hangs lush green curtains over the cliff face and in so doing helps to prevent the erosion of soil. There is also a succulent pelargonium or geranium, a cissus, a euphorbia and many others.

As you might expect, if you are a good botanist you can identify the family to which an unfamiliar succulent belongs by its flower. But even without being very knowledgeable about plants you can easily identify a cactus if the plant is in bloom, for the flowers are not produced on stems like others you know, but are sessile. The petals always grow from the top of an immature berry. Incidentally, some berries become ripe and always look good enough to eat. Don't worry if you have young children in the house, the fruits are both delicious and wholesome. I have been told that cactus-berry jam is the most delicious in the world, but my plants have never produced sufficient to fill the tiniest saucepan so I cannot speak from experience.

Some cacti have the prettiest flowers I know, but you can have a plant for years without ever having the pleasure of seeing it bloom. One of ours is nearly twenty years old and still hasn't flowered. But once a plant does flower then it is likely to bloom regularly. Furthermore, due to improved methods of cultivation, some house plant specialists such as Thomas Rochford are now marketing cacti in full bloom under the name of 'Flowers of the Desert'. It is very pleasing to be able to choose a cactus for its flower as well as for its general appearance.

Some of the blooms are large and showy and quite unbelievably beautiful, wonderful enough to have you rushing to your neighbour to come and admire your plant. Others are tiny, drab and undistinguished. Some nestle down among the woolly hairs on the plant like tiny daisies in the grass. Some flowers are produced singly and often one gorgeous bloom seems to be as much as the plant can produce, but other plants will produce a perfect ring of flowers around their heads. These, mammilaria, are known as garland cacti because of this habit, and they will sometimes produce a colourful mixture of flowers and bright berries intermingled, from the previous crop of bloom. Often the larger blooms are very short lived.

If you take an interest in cacti you can find them marvellously varied and their study can prove to be absolutely fascinating. There are a great many cacti enthusiasts, some of whom enjoy swapping species in the same way that stamp collectors exchange their duplicates. In this book I must deal with beginners and not enthusiasts, so I say quite simply that there are three distinct tribes and many sub-tribes.

In Tribe 1 are some plants which really do not look at all like cacti, but rather resemble any other shrubby plant. These are the Pereskieae. They are of value to the cactus enthusiast not so much for their worth as decorative plants as for their value as stock upon which other cacti can be grafted. For example, the leaf-flowering cacti are usually grafted on to these when someone wishes to make a 'standard' plant of them.

Tribe 2 has members which are possibly the most familiar to the layman, for in this group is the prickly pear of the genus opuntia, the name being an allusion to its luscious fruits. It is a large genus and the opuntias do not all resemble each other, for although many are flattened like the prickly pear, although smaller, others are rounded and very different in appearance.

In Tribe 3 are the plants which have the fabulous flowers, Cereae, the cereus cacti. Many of these are known as the night-blooming cacti because the funnel-like flowers bloom mainly during the hours of darkness. I once heard of a couple who threw a party on the night their one special cereus was expected to bloom. Many of these cacti are columnar in shape. There are many sub-tribes, most of which have tongue-twisting names. In one of the sub-tribes is the old man cactus, *Cephalocereus senilis*. Instead of the spines which are a characteristic of most cacti, the old man has long white hairs which cover the plant.

The sub-tribes contain some extra ordinary and fascinating plants. There is the astrophytum or star cactus, which is ridged or divided so that the plants resemble a blown-up star. The blooms grow as an attractive top-knot, usually one great open flower or sometimes a group of smaller ones. Barrel cacti are fun and can grow to a great size. Hedgehog cacti are round and very spiny, as you would expect. Peanut cactus, chamaecereus, looks like a prickly peanut, but it sprouts pretty red flowers.

Cacti only occur naturally in America, although they have been imported to all parts of the world. In some places some species, like the prickly pear for example, have become so much at home that one can be forgiven for believing them to be indigenous to those parts. Most of the species are terrestial and generally speaking these are the ones we most easily recognise as cacti. However, there are others which are epiphytes and which differ so much in appearance from the rest that many people are surprised to learn that they are indeed cacti. In my experience the most popular misconception on the part of the non-plantsman is that the epiphytic species are some kind of orchid, which is not so, of course.

These kinds come from warmer, moister regions than the desert flowers and so they do not need the same water-filled bodies. Naturally they have to be treated differently when they are grown as house plants.

They are the epiphyllums or leaf-flowering cactus, so called because the flattened stems on which the flowers are produced look more like leaves than stems. Many of them are grown in homes all over the world, for they are easy plants and they can produce masses of the most gorgeous and colourful flowers. They are also more decorative than the other types. Probably the best known of them is the so-called Christmas cactus, with its brilliantly coloured flowers which always remind me of Christmas tree baubles. I have more to say about these epiphyllums later.

As with most other house plants we have to come to terms with cacti and try to give them much the same conditions as they would have in their native environment. Where they live naturally they are accustomed to long periods of drought during which time they make little growth, indeed, are almost dormant. When a short but flooding rainy season occurs the plant makes up for lost time, grows and blooms, and at the same time stores up enough moisture in its fleshy body to see it through the next period of drought.

Fortunately it is fairly easy for us to provide more or less similar conditions at home if we turn the short, cool days of winter into the drought period. During this time it is sufficient to give the plants only the merest drink, just eonugh to moisten the soil surface, and then only about once a month. As the days grow longer and the light and sun more intense, we can increase the supply and water them once a week.

And as these are desert plants it stands to reason that they are very much used to sun, that they need it in fact, and as much as they can get. For this reason they should never be set back in a room away from the window light. There is one exception to this rule, that of the epiphytic cacti, but more of these later.

You do not need a very warm atmosphere to grow most cacti. In the desert the temperature often drops very low during the night and so like most desert plants cacti can tolerate a low temperature though not frost.

If you are fortunate enough to get your plants to flower remember that they should be rested after flowering. For about six weeks give them only sufficient water to prevent the soil from drying out completely.

There are so many cacti that I could fill a book with these alone. No wonder that these plants have their enthusiasts, for they are the collector's dream! Not only can you gradually amass a great natural variety of plants, but should you wish you can mould some of them to your own fancy, for it is quite possible to graft one type on to another.

One of the things that endears cacti to me is that these are such splendid plants to use for making miniature gardens of all kinds. I have filled many kinds of containers, from deep soup plates to discarded flower arrangement troughs and bowls with them. These arrangements make acceptable presents for all kinds of people, young and old, rich or poor. It is well to remember that when you are repotting, transplanting or even handling the body of a cactus plant that you should protect your fingers in some way, either by wearing gloves or by wrapping a cloth or piece of folded newspaper around the plant. Some of the spines, although very small, are very difficult to remove from the skin and can be painful for days. If you do find that you have collected some, try using a piece of Sellotape to remove them. Wrap this over the spine and then pull it smartly away. Usually the tiny spine or spines will come away with it.

If you use cacti to fill bowls see that they are watered first so that the root ball binds together well. Try to disturbe the roots as little as possible. The best way to water a miniature garden is gently to immerse it in a bowl of water so that the soil surface is just under the water.

You can buy cactus soil or compost ready mixed from most good garden shops. Alternatively mix your own by using equal parts of heavy loam, coarse sand, broken brick and old mortar rubble. The last may not always be easy to find, but my advice is that the thing to do is to haunt an area where old buildings are being demolished. Cacti do not require a rich, water-retentive soil. In their own environment they so often grow in sand which although it may be rich in minerals and plant foods has no leafmould or humus worth mentioning.

Therefore these plants are not equipped to deal with a rich soil mixture, nor one which has been designed to hold water. Neither are they adapted to deal with organisms that live in rotting leaves. So it really is important to get the correct compost for them.

If you would like to increase your stock you will find most cacti are quite easy to propagate. They root readily from either cuttings, offsets or side shoots, and as I said earlier it is possible to graft some kinds. But not all send out offsets or side shoots readily. One pleasant way of raising a little collection is from seed. Germination often takes a long time, perhaps because we cannot faithfully reproduce the natural conditions needed, the time depending upon the species.

Fortunately the seeds are fairly large, so they can be sown singly. It is useful to write down on the label the number of seeds you have sown, so that you know later whether or not there are more to appear. Be patient and retain the seed box and contents long after the first few have germinated so you do not throw away any seeds that are late in germinating.

For seed you need containers with a good layer of drainage material, crushed brick or charcoal pieces are excellent. Standard seed boxes or seed pans are usually best. If you do not buy a seed sowing compost for cacti, mix well two parts of loam, one part of fine peat and one part of sand. Moisten, but do not soak this compost before sowing the seed. Space out the seeds and cover them lightly with compost. Place the container in a plastic bag to ensure that the compost remains moist and place it in a temperature of 18–24° C., or 65–75° F. If you use a special propagating case, and there are many neat and helpful types suitable for the indoor gardener on the market, sow the seeds in February. You can also start them germinating in an airing cupboard or near a radiator, but failing these means of providing warmth wait until May before sowing the seed.

So far as mature plants are concerned, do not be in a hurry to repot these. I know that a cactus pot often looks too small for its plant, but wait until you are quite sure that the roots are overcrowded. Young plants are more likely to want repotting and if you grow your own from seed these may need constant moving on until they settle down to a slower growth. Large specimens can usually stay in their pots for three or four years, or even longer. Repot in the spring.

Although cacti often look top-heavy they do not normally tend to overbalance as a more leafy plant might. Earlier on I explained the advantages of placing a top-heavy pot inside a larger pot and plunging it in peat at the same time. Cacti will not need plunging, but I think that it is a good plan to sink them inside a cover pot rather than to stand their pots on a saucer. Not only do they look more attractive this way, but you are also not so likely to splash the water on the furniture or window sills.

Cacti enjoy a spell out of doors in summer. A rain shower or two seems to improve their condition and appearance. Place them in a sheltered spot so that they are not blown about, and keep an eye open for slugs, snails or other pests that you would not normally find indoors.

Unlike the other cacti, the epiphyllums do not like intense sunshine. They thrive best in a shady room which gets late afternoon sun. My own best specimens grow a few feet back from a west window. These cacti do not need such a definite resting period as the others. They also require more water, more humidity and a richer soil. They are best repotted in late summer, August or September. If you want to mix your own compost use three parts of well rotted leafmould, one part of loam, one part of sharp sand and a little sprinkling of bonemeal.

These cacti are very easy to increase. Many of my friends go away from my home clutching a 'leaf' from one of my plants, and I also continuously root cuttings so that there are always a few plants growing up. Like any cactus that has a jointed stem (opuntias are others), you can sever the stem at the joint and use the severed piece as a cutting. It is best never to take the cuttings during the peak growing season. Instead, take them some eight weeks before or after this. Strangely, I think, cactus cuttings appear to root best in dry peat, but epiphyllums root quickest in a moist mixture of chopped sphagnum moss and peat.

I cannot enthuse enough over the great beauty of the epiphyllums. These really are wonderfully decorative plants. I like to arrange my plants so that they are above eye level so that we can fully appreciate the beauty of the downward curving stems. When a plant displayed this way is in bloom it is a mass of colour. The flowers are gorgeous and some of them, according to the species or variety, are very large. Some plants will produce very many blooms, even hundreds. So many hybrids have been raised that there really are thousands of named epiphyllums or 'orchid' cacti. The colours range from violet, red, pink, orange and yellow to pure white.

You may find many other types sold under a variety of names other than 'orchid' cactus. The Easter cactus is *Schlumbergera gaertneri*. It has bright red flowers borne on the end of its 'leaves', and it much resembles the Christmas cactus. This, actually, is a name given to two species, most frequently to *Zygocactus truncatus*, but also to *Schlumbergera bridgesii*. The first of the two is also called Thanksgiving cactus and Crab cactus, a reference to the shape of its 'leaves'.

If you would like to astonish your friends and gain a reputation for growing fabulous flowers try to get a specimen of *Nopalxochia phyllanthoides* and grow it in a hanging basket in a shady window. You will be thrilled as the succession of beautiful carmine-rose flowers grow from the lovely, flattened, pendant stems with wavy, scalloped margins.

12. The Many Names of Crassula

As I said in the previous chapter, a succulent might be just one odd man out in any family of plants, adapted to take advantage of the environment in which it naturally grows. However, there is one great and glorious family, Crassulaceae, in which all the members, both shrubs and herbs, are succulents. Its name describes the plant well, for it comes from the Latin word *crassus,* which means thick, a reference to the character of the leaves.

Many of the plants in this family are beautiful even when not in flower. They would appeal especially to those who shy away from the prickly and often even harsh exteriors of many cacti. A great number of them grow in the form of rosettes and resemble individual blooms of thick, often beautifully marked, petals. In some cases the flowers of these plants are apparently not particularly distinctive, although I have found that even the most seemingly undistinguished inflorescences are rewarding if you care to examine them through a lens. They are then found to be lovely, strange, vividly coloured, or of unusual shapes. There are others, such as the echeverias, whose bell-shaped flowers are larger, sometimes long-stemmed, really gorgeous and unlike any other flowers we grow. In the market in spring stems are sometimes sought by clever and imaginative florists because they are so unusual and so long lasting.

Some of the plant rosettes sit on the soil surface but there are others which are borne on long stout stems. Often such a plant will produce several rosettes on a thick 'trunk' and so make a handsome and distinctive plant.

Among these is a plant which I heartily recommend to beginners. It is *Aeonium tabulaeforme.* Among the crassulaceae are many plants highly treasured by connoisseurs who can give them skilled attention under greenhouse conditions. Most of the aeoniums fall into this class, but by no means all of them. *A. tabulaeforme* is a species which is very easy to grow and does not like too warm conditions. The first one I knew lived on a windowsill in a farmer neighbour's house, and there it grew and grew and flowered most handsomely, finally becoming the mother plant of many other aeoniums which gradually appeared on other windowsills about the district.

Its thick, beautifully formed, light green leaves, 100 to 200 to a rosette, have a pleasing healthy sheen. A mature plant will produce attractive flowering spikes, their stout stems growing to one or two feet, the top half becoming very branching and bearing stems of masses of long-lasting pale yellow flowers, each about two thirds of an inch across.

Although we shall return to the subject of plant rosettes, let us first take a moment to discuss some of the other highly individualistic plants in this particular family. If you are fascinated by plant oddities I think that you would be sure to enjoy growing living stones or adromischus. The name is from adros, strong, and miskos, a stem, and it is said to refer to the stout flower stem. I think that the botanist must have been at a loss for a name, for the flowers are the least part of the plant's appeal and attraction. I would have expected the inspiration for the name to have come from the thick, fleshy leaves. These are wonderfully marbled and patterned. The plants possess a particular static quality, an interesting example of plant camouflage, I imagine. Adromischus are unusual rather than decorative. They are easy to grow and should be treated like cacti. They are in sufficient variety for one to be able to build up a collection and offer any plantsman, young or old, an interesting hobby.

Also chunky and often marbled, but also strikingly and fantastically frilled and margined with colour, or patterned and covered with a silver grey bloom or meal, are plants in another group of crassulaceae, the cotyledons.

How confusing some horticultural terms and names can be!

D

This cotyledon has nothing to do with seed leaves. The name comes from kotyle, a cavity, in the leaves of a plant. The particular plant, *Cotyledon umbilicus,* once gave its name to the family. Now, even more confusingly, it is known as *Umbilicus pedulinus* and has severed its connection with the old name.

This is a trying race altogether, so far as synonyms go. Many of the plants in the cotyledon genus are likely to be found masquerading as echeverias, sedums and rosularias. It doesn't really matter to the non-botanist, I suppose, for one is more likely to buy a plant because of the beauty of its leaves or its flowers than for its correct label, no matter how quaint. But if you take plant collecting seriously then this is a different matter.

I grow many plants from this great tribe, for like cacti they are so good for planting in groups in a variety of containers. Most of the time I mix them, but occasionally one plant will reproduce itself so generously that I am able to fill one container with one kind. A large bowl filled with succulent rosettes can be extremely lovely and placed on a low table so that one can look into it, both decorative and pleasing. Cotyledons are ideal for helping one to make a striking arrangement. They should be handled with extreme care, like others such as echeverias, otherwise the soft, mealy surface of the leaves can become spoiled by markings. Incidentally, when watering plants with a bloom or meal, avoid dropping water on their surfaces, for this can also mark them. The plants in crassulaceae are sufficiently varied for anyone to be able to fill many containers with different textures, shapes and sizes.

Most of my bowls are stood outside in the summer and brought in before the frosts threaten. They are then given the sunniest positions we can provide. They do not demand great heat and the minimum temperature in which they should be grown is about 5–7° C., or 40–45° F. Our own rooms are normally kept at about 18–20° C., or 65–70° F. during winter. Good light is essential.

The soil must be well drained and water given only in moderation. Actually, if you keep the soil on the dry side the leaf colour is intensified. However, dryness of the soil can also cause some of the lower leaves to fall prematurely. If the sight of a portion of bare stem offends, it is possible to cut off the neat top and root this. It roots quite readily. I discovered this by accident and what pleased me most was that not only did I have a nice new rosette growing neatly, but the bare stem left in the pot also sprouted!

All of these plants are extremely easy to propagate by stem or leaf cuttings, according to the nature of the plant. Sometimes even a fallen leaf will root and make a new plant.

Many of the plants which carry the family name have pretty flowers, some of them delightfully scented. However, one of the plants I have had for many years, *Crassula argentea.* the jade plant, has never flowered although it is now well over a foot high and resembles a little Japanese tree with glossy chunky leaves. Its flowers when they do appear will be in pink pannicles borne on the tips of the stems. This plant will go on for decades and will in time make a fine 'tree' with a thick, stout stem or trunk. There is some confusion over synonyms here, by the way. *C. argentea,* possibly because it is tree-like, is often wrongly labelled *C. arborescens,* and to balance the situation, *C. arborescens* is called *C. argentea!* But both are well worth growing.

Labelled *Cotyledon coccinea, Crassula coccinea, C. rubicunda* and *Kalosanthes coccinea* is a charming, fragrant, flowering plant which is actually *Rochea coccinea.* All the plants in the crassulaceae have opposite leaves and in the rochea these are so close that they give the plant the appearance of having the chunky leaves threaded on the stem in pairs, one pair pointing in the opposite direction to the pair above and below.

Also scented, and doubly welcome since the flowers bloom in the darkest days of winter, are the kalanchoes, which are similar to the rocheas in appearance. These also like a well-drained soil and they need a little more water than those we have already discussed, plenty in summer but rather less in winter, even though the plant may be flowering. Generally speaking, these plants are a little more tender and the minimum temperature for them should not be allowed to fall below about 10° C., or 50° F.

I like to feed them while they are receiving plenty of water, but before they begin to make their flower buds, and certainly before they actually come into bloom. If you try to feed a plant while it is receiving little water it may become scorched. Kalanchoes are plants which flower best when kept in a small pot. If you give them too much room they will make foliage at the expense of the flowers. After they have flowered, prune them. Cut each plant down, quite drastically. This will promote the flower growth for the next season.

I have a beautiful little variegated plant, *Kalanchoe fedts-chenkoi* 'Marginata' with leaves most beautifully coloured in grey-green and cream and margined with rosy-magenta, the young, growing tip being often flushed as well. Its creamy-green blooms are not distinguished, but its leaves are as pretty as any flower. The silver-grey *K. fedtchenkoi* is also hand-some, and it is a species I like to use in mixed arrangements, for it grows tall yet remains quite dainty. Cuttings grown in tiny containers and slightly starved in consequenece have a delightfully miniature air.

Some flowering kalanchoes can be easily grown from seed on a warm windowsill. Varieties such as Brilliant Star, scarlet; Morning Sun, gold; Tetra Vulcan, a lovely red, are examples. Sow the seed in spring or summer for flowers the following winter.

Some of the most delightful flowers I know are those coral red bells, tipped and lined with bright yellow, one to three to a dainty stem, which are produced by the shrubby oliveranthus, *Echeveria harmsii*. This also can be raised from seed. It flowers in spring and is well worth growing but is not quite so easy as some.

Echeverias are among the most beautiful and fascinating of all pot plants. You may have seen some of them, silvery-grey roses, later sprouting coral flowers, sitting on the soil around the edges of some splendid flower bed in a park or formal flower bed in a garden. But there are many more than these summer-flaunted *E. gibbiflora* 'Metallica'. Gibbiflorus means that they have 'humped' flowers. One could set out to make a collection of echeverias alone and find enough to do to fill all the days.

The leaves are always in rosettes and although many are grey and covered with a lovely bloom, some are covered with plush instead. One is so plushy that it is called the woolly rose. They have fascinating flowers, usually coral, scarlet, yellow or white. Indoors they often bloom at a time when other flowers are scarce. They can be grown in just the same easy way as cotyledons, and some seedsmen stock the seed.

There are more of the crassulaceae to delight you, including sedums, many of which are hardy and grow in our gardens, and I must leave you to your own explorations, but before I leave this tribe let me introduce you to one which has enchanted people for centuries. It is bryophyllum, from *bryo,* to sprout, and *phyllon,* a leaf. If you see a plant you will soon understand why it received this name. You might think at first glance that the large, opposite leaves are fringed in a very distinctive way, and so they are, but look again! What seems at first glance to be a border of frills of a deeper tone turns out to be a leaf edging of tiny plantlets which form between the teeth of the leaves. Some of them even have tiny root hairs attached and as the little plantlets fall from the parent leaf on to the soil in the pot below these hairs quickly root and establish a new and growing plant. They can, of course, be detached by hand and planted according to your wishes instead of the whim of the plant.

These plants like a rich soil and plenty of water during the summer. They also like a warm environment, with a minimum temperature of about 10° C., or 50° F.

Once again, as with so many members of this family, some plants get labelled differently. This time bryophyllums are sometimes called kalanchoe, but if they are flowering you should be able to sort them out. The flowers of bryophyllums are pendulous, while the others grow erect. The species you are most likely to find on sale is known for obvious reasons as mother of thousands, and is *B. daigremontianum.*

You have seen how easy it is to increase bryophyllums, but

as you may have gathered by descriptions of other plants, succulents are usually extremely easy to increase. Often you will find that a plant of one species has dropped on to the soil in the pot of another kind and has started growing away quite happily.

If you want to increase one of your plants have ready a little pot of either silver sand or cutting compost. Pull off a leaf and press its base a little way into the surface. Water it in and after this withhold the water until you can tell by a gentle tugging that the leaf has rooted. After a while tiny leaves will begin to grow at the base of the mother leaf.

If you have a succulent which produces offshoots these may be detached and planted. The members of the crassula family seem most eager to root under almost all circumstances. I once found a discarded flower stem sending out both roots and shoots. It is interesting and entertaining to make a mixture of these leaf cuttings in a bowl and watch how they grow into a pleasant miniature garden.

Finally, if you seek horticultural entertainment, buy a packet of mixed succulent seeds. In one seedsman's catalogue I see that among the 20 kinds of seed in the packet you can expect to find agave, aloe, anacapseros, argyroderma, cotyledon, echeveria, faucaria, gasteria, gibbaeum, haworthia, rochea, etc. Not all crassulaceae by all means, but a fine start to a collection – and a cheap one!

13. Bulbs are Nature's Prepacks

If you have never grown a plant in your life then you could not do better than begin in autumn with a spring-flowering bulb, and a hyacinth for preference. Although its natural element is the soil, like many of the other plants you have met a hyacinth will grow in plain water with just a little charcoal to keep it sweet. Other flowers can also be grown this way, but probably the easiest and certainly the best example is the hyacinth.

It is possible to buy special hyacinth glasses. These are specially designed with a flared portion at the top in which a single bulb will sit firmly. You can grow a hyacinth in the top of any glass which will hold it, but you should make certain that it cannot easily be knocked off. When the plant blooms it will be quite heavy, and if the bulb is not properly supported it will be unbalanced.

The bulb should not sit in the water but its base should be just above the surface. You will find that the roots will gradually grow down from the base of the bulb into the water until in time they fill the glass. Keep a watch, and top up the water level when necessary.

Much of the success in growing spring-flowering bulbs lies in looking after them properly in the early days. It is best for any bulb to be in the dark until the roots are growing well. It is also important that the dark place should be cool. In a way one tries to reproduce the conditions the bulbs would be growing under were they planted outdoors in the garden. I have been shown bulbs that never grew properly and when I made enquiries have found that they had been started off in a dark cupboard right enough, but sometimes it was one which was next to the chimney, or one through which hot water pipes passed. Look for a *cool,* dark place.

If no cupboard or other covered place is available and you have to grow the bulbs on your windowsill, then it might be best to keep them outside rather than inside the glass to begin with, if this is safe. You could, perhaps, stand the hyacinth glass or glasses inside a covered box there. Alternatively use a black plastic bag or some sheeting. When I was a child and bedrooms were cold we kept our hyacinth glasses on the bedroom windowsills and covered each one with a dunce cap cone made of dark paper.

The cover should remain on until, during one of your routine inspections, you can see the roots are beginning to grow quickly. Usually by this time the little shoot will be showing in the nose of the bulb also, looking like a tiny pearl. The cover can be removed at this point, but do not bring the bulb into a very much warmer place. Keep it on the coolest or least sunny windowsill. You can now have the pleasure of seeing it grow, and the slower it grows the better will be the flowers. You can bring it into a warmer place when the flower spike is well coloured although still in bud. Each day turn the glass a little so that all sides of the new plant get their ration of direct daylight. This will help it to grow upright and even.

Some people grow hyacinths no other way than in glasses. However, you can also grow them in water and pebbles and planted in bulb fibre or in one of the soil-less composts we use for our house plants.

Many of the narcissi will also grow splendidly this way. Indeed, some of them grow better in pebbles than in pots of soil. The variety 'Cragford' is one of these. If you would like many pots of spring flowering bulbs send for a catalogue from a good bulb merchant. In it you will find the kinds and varieties listed, with details of which will force well and which are best grown outdoors. There is a good choice available. Trumpet daffodils and the many-flowered polyanthus types will grow well indoors.

If you grow bulbs in bowls of pebbles, use some charcoal among the stones just as I recommended for puddle pots. Half fill the bowl with pebbles, stand the bulbs on the surface and wedge them upright with the pebbles where necessary. See that their noses come well above the rim of the bowl. The bulbs can be as close as you like so long as they do not touch each other. Allow about an inch between the surface of the pebbles and the rim of the container. Pour in the water so that it comes just below the bulb bases. Keep it topped up to this level.

It is possible to have a house filled with growing flowers through the darkest days of winter by cultivating many kinds of spring-flowering bulbs. The easiest of all are hyacinths. The earliest of these are much smaller than the fat and luscious-looking spikes that one grows in glasses. These are the Roman or Multiflora types which produce more than one stem to a bulb, each stem with only a few flowers. They are valuable in that they flower very early, in time for Christmas, without having to be treated in some special way by the bulb merchant. Many bulbs are specially treated so that they will flower early. These are a little more expensive. They must be planted by a certain date and according to the bulb merchant's directions.

The little flowers of the Roman hyacinths look delightful when massed. Try a large washbasin planted thick with them for a special winter treat. In addition to their dainty appearance they give off a particularly sweet and welcome perfume.

When we grow bulbs indoors we 'force' them into early bloom. Forced bulbs cannot usually be grown a second year with good results. So, as a rule, forced bulbs are either discarded or planted in the garden. Here they will slowly recover and in time bloom well again.

If you get them planted early enough, as soon as they appear in the shops or are delivered by the bulb merchant, you can force Roman hyacinths into bloom in November. If you would like a succession of flowers it is best to plant bulbs at intervals. Do not mix kinds or varieties, otherwise you might find them flowering at different times. This might sound a good plan, but actually it is not. Once a bulb has flowered and begins to fade it is quite unsightly. If all the plants in one bowl do not flower at the same time you will have faded plants hanging around waiting for the others to bloom and giving the entire bowl a tired appearance.

Also flowering very early, before Christmas, are two nice, old-fashioned, highly fragrant narcissi: 'Paper White' and the yellow 'Soleil d'Or'. Following these fairly rapidly according to the time you plant them, are others of the polyanthus or Tazetta type narcissi such as the double 'Cheerfulness', the bright centred 'Geranium' and the creamy 'Cragford'. Next come the large types, daffodils such as 'Carlton', 'King Alfred', 'Double Texas' and the pure white 'Mount Hood', to mention just a few. If you like scented flowers you can grow some of the jonquils.

Tulips are not really plants for the beginner since they take a little more skill in forcing. The easiest of all are the double early varieties and these can be grown in bulb fibre, soil-less composts and in soil, but not in water.

Bulb fibre is on sale in most garden shops. If you wish to mix your own you will need six parts by bulk of peat, two parts of crushed oyster shell and one part of crushed charcoal. All these ingredients will be found on sale in garden shops. Be sure to mix them thoroughly together and moisten the fibre before planting. Test for moisture by taking up a handful and squeezing it. No water should be squeezed out, and the resulting ball of bulb fibre should adhere together instead of crumbling. When you plant see that all the bulb noses are above the soil level. This ensures that water does not settle in their centres and rot them, for they will require watering occasionally while the bulbs are growing their roots. If they are out of sight in some dark place and in the cool, do not allow them to go out of mind. Make sure that they are inspected from time to time.

Containers can be as varied as you wish. I use the traditional bulb bowls, but I also use many other vessels from flower arrangement containers to casseroles, wash basins and anything else that appeals to me and will blend well with the flowers that are about to be produced. Most bulbs will grow quite well in shallow vessels, but it is wise to reserve these for low-growing kinds. Those which become tall and heavy will be inclined to flop about. These really need a deep root hold. As a very general rule, try to use containers at least twice the depth of the length of the bulbs which are to go in them.

Do remember that all spring-flowering bulbs must be kept cool and dark in the early stages. When the roots are growing and the tiny shoot is showing bring them into the house by degrees, keeping them in the coolest places first and only gradually introducing them into the warmth of the living rooms. Never let the fibre or compost become dry at any time after the bulbs have been planted.

If you have no cellar, shed or other cool, dark place large enough to take several bowls, keep them outside against the north side of the house. Wrap them in black plastic sheeting, or enclose them in black plastic bags. Inspect them from time to time, and watch out for mice. Field mice will sometimes eat some kinds of bulbs.

I have stressed the fact that the plants we have just discussed are spring-flowering types because there are many other lovely plants which can be grown indoors from bulbs and which will flower at other times of the year.

Perhaps the best known and certainly the most gorgeous of these is a plant known popularly as amaryllis, although in fact it should be called a hippeastrum. The amaryllis is the belladonna lily which flowers in the garden.

These are again sometimes specially prepared by the bulb merchant and sold out of season, and as always such bulbs must be treated and grown according to the directions which come with them. Hippeastrums are extremely easy to grow and the show they put on is positively theatrical!

Pot the bulbs in January, one bulb to a pot. The bulbs are quite large. Choose a pot which will allow about an inch of soil all around the bulb. Plant it so that one third of the bulb, its nose area, is above soil level. Allow also about an inch between the soil surface and the pot rim, because you will need to water the plant freely once growth begins. The flower spike usually appears before the foliage. Once you see it, feed the plant with a good soluble plant food. When the flower fades cut off the faded bloom head but leave the stem. Gradually give a little less water as you see the leaves begin to fade, until at last the plant is receiving no water at all when the leaves have died down. From this point allow the bulb to go quite dry, so that it can rest and ripen. Remove the dry and faded leaves and stem. Repot the bulb next year, and repeat the process.

Lilies can be grown in pots and it is possible to force them into bloom, although I would not really suggest that this is a beginner's pastime. However, there are today specially prepared lilies which are very easy to grow, some coming complete and planted in a pot so that water alone needs to be added. Prepared lilies can be bought from bulb merchants and garden shops, and I can thoroughly recommend them.

One of the prettiest and certainly one of the easiest of all 'bulbs' is a pretty little garden orchid which does extremely well as a house plant. It is called bletia or blettilla. You can buy the pseudo-bulbs from any good bulb merchant. Potting is simplicity itself. I grow mine in one of the soil-less composts, Kerimure. Plant the bulbs in March simply by pressing them into the surface of the compost. I plant five or six bulbs together in one container. In about six weeks the orchids flower, sending up pretty little spikes of magenta-coloured blooms. They need plenty of water, keeping the compost considerably wetter than for most plants, and as this is so there is a danger of an unpleasant odour unless a few nuggets of charcoal are incorporated in the drainage material in the bowl.

Once the blooms die down the leaves begin to grow more vigorously. At this time they can either be stood outdoors in a sheltered place or in a frame, or indoors on a north-facing windowsill. Those placed outdoors should be brought inside in about August and kept on a shady windowsill. During this time they should be watered only moderately until October. From then until March the bulbs should be given no water, so that they can become rested and ripened. In March they should be repotted and the process begun again. These little flowers are so pretty and cultivation is so simple that anyone can grow them. They are surprisingly inexpensive for so gorgeous and luxurious a flower.

There are many other flowering bulbs which can be grown indoors, and I ought, perhaps, to make it quite clear that I use the term 'bulbs' loosely to cover also such similar beginnings as corms and tubers. You can buy a wonderful assortment from any good merchant. I find that the study of one of the several well illustrated catalogues is a stimulating experience. There are always so many things that I want to grow and I try to have something new each year. As I said earlier, the introduction of more and more specially prepared bulbs makes their cultivation almost foolproof, so long as one follows the simple directions carefully. But by no means are all bulbs yet in this category.

Eucomis bicolor is known as the pineapple flower because of the way its little flowers are arranged at the end of the thick stem. These are surmounted, like the pineapple, with a tuft of leaves. Indeed, the name comes from eukomes, beautiful haired! The flowers are sweetly scented and this really is a delightful plant. It needs a temperature of only about 7° C., 45° F., in winter, so you can see that it is not demanding. In fact, eucomis will grow outdoors in a sheltered garden or a warm climate. It grows best in a light, warm home. The bulbs should be planted in March, one to a five-inch pot, so if you want to grow three or more together, take a guide to the container size from this.

Water them very moderately from March until May, and then increase the quantity or the frequency until the plants are being watered freely. Taper off again in September and water very little until March comes around again. Begin feeding them occasionally with a soluble plant food once the flower spike shows.

Many bulbous plants which can be pot grown produce some most interesting and distinctive flowers and are just the thing for those who like to propagate a little wonder in their lives. In the window of one antique shop in the West Country each year there stands an enormous and quite beautiful bowl containing several blood lilies. It is interesting to note from a distance just how many people, passers-by, stop and stare at the flowers, obviously wondering what they can be. The plant produces long broad leaves from which rise the showy, red blooms in a dense, globular head. Like the hippeastrums or amaryllis, these flowers come from bulbs which should be planted at only half their depth, noses well out of the soil. You can plant several in one container and they flower best if they are left undisturbed for three or four years. They can be increased easily from offsets. Also like the hippeastrums, the bulbs must be rested in some dry and sunny place, on a shelf or in a frame. This period of ripening really is important. Water very little until you see that growth is beginning, and then increase the amount. When the plants begin to flower start to feed them with a very weak food solution once a week or so. When they begin to fade gradually decrease the watering rate. Once again, these plants are almost hardy and do not need a temperature above about 7° C. in winter.

The real difficulty, I find, is being able to buy the bulbs. One must be an opportunist in this case, and either beg some offsets or make exhaustive enquiries of bulb merchants. This may be a nuisance, but the curious flowers are well worth growing – and seeking! Ask for haemanthus if the common name is not enough.

The same applies to hymenocallis. The lovely white flowers of *H. calathina* open in succession, filling the air around them with their sweet scent. Pot the bulbs in March (you can detach offsets at this stage). Leave them undisturbed for three or four years. Keep them quite dry from December to April. The bulbs usually start growing in late April or May and they can then be fed once or twice a week, but keep the solution very weak. Grow them in a sunny place.

Sprekelia formosissima, the Jacobean lily (I think that it must get its name because it looks like the vivid scarlet 'lilies' in Jacobean embroidery) is easily bought, I am happy to say. Give the bulbs the same treatment as you did your hippeastrums.

Although they are recommended as plants to grow outdoors in the garden, acidanthera also do well in pots. I first grew them outdoors in pots on a roof garden in the heart of London, so you can see that they should have no mollycoddling. The flowers are closely related to the gladiolus, but they differ somewhat in appearance, being more starry and with a dark central blotch. They also have an exquisite perfume. They flower from August until late October. Plant them from late March to early May, five corms to a six-inch pot. Keep them on a windowsill in good light.

From the bulb merchant you can also buy anomatheca, which apparently should really be called *Lapeirousia cruenta*. This also is a little plant which grows happily outdoors in a warm rock garden, and it will make a charming show of crimson flowers in summer. Mass the bulbs in pots from September onwards. Keep them outdoors, covered, until growth begins and then bring them into the warmth. Water them moderately. Let them dry off after flowering and keep them dry until potting time comes around again.

Nerines are among some of the most beautiful of all bulb flowers, with wonderful colour and graceful shapes. Pot them at any time from August to November, half in and half out of the soil. They look best grouped in threes or fives in a six-inch pot, or larger. Be sure to provide a good layer of drainage material, for this is essential with these bulbs. They will grow outdoors in a sunny border, so they will not need heat indoors, but they must have good light. Grow them in much the same way as hippeastrum, except that these will not need potting anew each year. The important thing to make sure of flowers the following year is to be sure to ripen them really well. If you have a greenhouse keep the pots on their sides high on a shelf near the glass roof where they will receive a good baking. Otherwise find some similar spot, even if this is no more than a dry box with a sheet of glass over it.

Although these are not technically bulbs, I feel I must include here lily-of-the-valley, or convallaria, which are among those plants which are specially prepared for easy forcing. We call the fat roots crowns rather than bulbs or corms. Once planted they grow very quickly indeed, and it is possible to plant them in successive batches so that you get the pretty, scented flowers all through the winter.

You can buy 'prepacks' from some firms, a few crowns

already planted in a little pot, and all you then have to do is follow the instructions on the packet.

Failing this, explain to the bulb merchant that you want the crowns for pot culture, and if you would like to try growing a succession mention this also, because they will then be sent to you from the cold store at different times.

Plant the crowns in deep bowls or pots with their tips just above the soil surface. Use a potting compost. Allow about two inches between the crowns. Water them well and place them in a *warm*, dark place (I use the airing cupboard). You will remember that most of the bulbs mentioned earlier have to go into a *cold*, dark place. If you have no such position, place the pot in a black plastic bag, inflate it so that there is air around the pot, and stand it near a radiator or cooker.

Another method of blacking out is to plant the crowns in a deep flower pot and turn an empty pot of equal size upside down on top of it. Put a cork or some other kind of plug in the drainage hole to exclude every bit of light. Although the soil must not be sodden it should be properly moist, for the crowns must not dry out during this period. Inspect them from time to time if you have any doubts on this question.

It does not take long under these conditions for the shoots to begin growing, usually about ten days. When they are about four inches tall bring them out, and each day move them just a little nearer to a window with good light. If you do this too quickly they will tend to mark time and begin to grow slowly and more naturally. Do not forget that you are forcing the flowers into bloom. Keep them well watered all the time they are growing.

If you would like a really simple and inexpensive method of producing flowers of the lily-of-the-valley, try this one. Place a two- to three-inch layer of moist peat at the bottom of a large black plastic bag. On the surface arrange the roots of the lilies and cover these with more peat leaving the tips just showing. Close the bag and stand it in a warm place. Inspect it from time to time, but do not leave it open for longer than you can help. This will obviously not produce the flowers in a pretty enough fashion for the living room, but if you wish to

have the flowers merely for cutting this is a good way to grow
them.

You cannot force these specially prepared crowns a second
time. They should either be planted in the garden where they
can recover at their leisure or they should be thrown away.

14. Flowering Plants in General

Once it is known that you are growing plants indoors you are sure to have more given to you! We all receive flowering plants, usually at Christmas time, but also at other times of the year. Don't be disappointed if you find that you cannot keep these growing well enough to bloom for another year. Circumstances may be against you. Usually, like forced bulbs, flowering plants have been grown out of their correct season.

I like to try to persuade indoor gardeners to regard most flowering plants as temporary tenants of their homes. In the first place quite a lot of them are annuals and once these have flowered, quite naturally they die. Some of them are perennials treated as annuals, and these expend their energies so freely that once they have flowered they usually are spent. Other perennials and some shrubs, azaleas for example, are not only forced into bloom but quite often at a time which is not, like bulbs, just a few weeks early but sometimes several months. In order to do this the grower will use photosynthetic processes involving subjecting the plants to artificial spells of short days, or short nights, as the case may be. This means that should the plant continue to live after it has finished flowering it is most unlikely to produce flowers again in the following year in the same months. It will need two or three years to become adjusted. Poinsettias are a good example of this.

Naturally we wish to keep our plants as long as possible. I hate throwing any away and am inclined to hang on to them long after they have ceased to look really attractive, but really it is best to be hard-hearted about this, and to treat a flowering plant more as though it were a bunch of flowers, one which has lasted better than usual.

If you have a greenhouse or a conservatory, sometimes the

plant can be taken from the house and given a convalescent period of better conditions for a year or two.

Obviously the most important thing is to know how to care for flowering plants while they are at their best. If they do so well with you that they go on living for a longer period than expected, then take this as a little bonus and be grateful, instead of trying to drag the last drops of value or satisfaction out of a plant which is old, ailing and ugly.

Let us now look briefly at a number of the most popular flowering plants. I shall take them alphabetically, rather than try to rate them in order either of importance or of decorative value.

Anthurium

This is an aeroid and so it will remain decorative even while it is not in flower. It needs a warm room and good light. The large green leaves need grooming if they are to continue to look handsome, so sponge them clean regularly. Water the plant only moderately in winter but more freely in summer. Large plants can be divided quite successfully.

You might like to try a new way to propagate your anthurium. Knock the plant from its pot and divide the roots. Plant up one or more sections in the normal manner, but keep one back. Wash the soil from the thong-like roots of this and rest the plant in the top of a hyacinth glass so that its crown is out of water but the roots are kept moist. Feed the waer from time to time, keeping the level constant. The plant will grow and thrive.

Azalea

Here is a plant which too often dies of drought. Never allow the root ball to dry out. Immediately you receive the plant stand the pot in a bucket of water, preferably rain water, with the soil surface just covered. Leave it there until there are no more air bubbles to be seen rising from the soil. Remove, drain and plunge it inside a cover pot filled with moist peat. It needs a warm home and good light, but not direct sunlight. Always use rain water if possible, if you live in a hard water area. When it is in flower bud feed it fortnightly and carry on feeding it for a little while after the flowers open. Pick off all the faded flowers as soon as they have passed their best. Repot the plant after it has finished flowering, using a size larger pot and pure peat rather than soil or any proprietary compost. Be sure to ram this peat around the old root ball very firmly, trying to get the same texture throughout. Syringe the foliage during hot, dry days, again using rain water. You can stand the plant outside in a partially shaded place in summer, preferably plunging the pot in a peat bed.

Begonia, large flowered

These plants grow from tubers. They need good light but should be kept out of direct sunlight. Water them freely in summer and feed them while they are in flower. As the flowers fade, gradually reduce the amount of water they receive until the soil is quite dry. The tuber must be rested during the winter. Leave it in its dry soil. Take it out in the early spring and start it growing again by putting it in a pot of moist peat or leafmould. Keep this moist but not sodden. The tuber must be kept in a warm place, about 19° or 20° C., or 65–70° F. When the roots are growing well transfer the tuber to a larger pot of good compost. Begin watering it a little more, and as growth increases add to the frequency or the quantity. Feed the plant when the flowers are seen to be forming. Fibrous-rooted begonias have smaller flowers. They need similar treatment, except that the plants do not die down.

Beloperone, or shrimp plant

Humidity is important to this plant, so keep it plunged. See that the plunge medium is always moist, rather than over-watering the soil in which the plant is growing. Give it maximum light, and feed regularly with a weak soluble plant food while it is in flower.

Cyclamen

This is a tremendously popular plant, and with good reason, but one also that frequently leaves much disappointment in its wake. It will die, or at least fail to flourish, if there are any fumes, gas, oil or smoke, in the air. Indications of poisoning are a quick yellowing and dropping of the leaves. It does not need a warm room, and a windowsill out of the sun is a good place for it, because it must have plenty of light. Plants are best plunged. If this is not done, be sure when you water to avoid allowing any to touch the top of the corm from which the leaves and flowers grow. If water collects there it is apt to set up a rotting that will soon kill the plant. The best way to water is to pour the water into the pot or saucer in which the plant pot sits and allow it to become absorbed. But do not let the plant sit constantly in a little pool, or it will drown. Let the soil become almost dry before re-watering. When the leaves and flowers fade gradually withhold water so that the corm can rest and ripen. Keep the soil almost but not quite dry during this period. At the end of summer remove the top inch or so of soil very gently and replace it with new. Begin to water again, moderately at first, until the leaves appear. Feed when the flower buds begin to show.

Erica or heather

Like the azaleas, the ericas are also grown in peat, and like them, too, ericas are most frequently killed by dryness at the roots and too dry air around them. Keep the soil constantly moist. These are really outdoor plants, so give them the cool and airy conditions they like without subjecting them to direct draughts. Use rain water both for watering and for spraying the foliage, which should be done at frequent intervals.

Euphorbia pulcherrima or poinsettia

Once again, the roots should be kept constantly moist without allowing the soil to become sodden. You must try to strike the happy medium. Like the cyclamen, euphorbia cannot live in a fume-polluted atmosphere. It needs good light, but must not be in direct and bright sunlight, especially that which shines through glass. An even temperature is essential. If you want to try to keep it growing, cut the stems right back after flowering, right down to the second bud from the base. Breeding and selecting has produced in recent years a strain of poinsettias which are much tougher and long-lasting than older varieties. You can now expect to keep a plant in good condition for several moths instead of the previous several weeks.

Gloxinia

These beautiful and exotic plants can sometimes be a little difficult. They are grown from tubers which you can sometimes keep and bring into growth in the next season. The plants need good light, but not sunlight. Rooms should be well ventilated, but beware of draughts. Be sure that the soil does not dry out at any time, but let it become almost dry before re-watering. Once again, make sure that no water lodges in the top of the tuber between the leaf stems, or these will tend to rot. Feed with a weak soluble food while the plant is in flower. Rest the tuber in winter and repot it in February.

Saintpaulia or African violet
This is still another plant which must have an unpolluted environment. It needs plenty of water in summer but careful and moderate watering in winter. Some warmth is essential, as is good light, but not direct sunlight. Try not to drop water on the leaves when you are watering, for these drops sometimes act like a magnifying glass and burn the leaf surface should sunlight shine through them. Plants are best plunged.

Streptocarpus
Give these plants plenty of light. They do not need very warm conditions. Water them freely from April to October and after this keep them almost dry. Feed them lightly when they are in flower. They like a well ventilated room, but plants should not be stood in a draught. Avoid dropping water on the leaves. Repot in spring.

These are the most popular of flowering plants and those which you are most likely to find on sale everywhere, but there are others which might come your way or perhaps which you might like to grow yourself. And here I would like to encourage any reader to try to grow on a windowsill any flowering plant which can be grown in the average greenhouse. Do not, however, attempt those which need a hot house with very high temperatures and great humidity.

I always have some flowering plants growing from seed. At the time of writing I am growing streptocarpus. These have so far spent their entire lives on a west-facing, but because of nearby trees, not really very sunny windowsill. I sow the seeds in low bowls and keep them inside plastic bags until the seedlings are large enough to handle. They are then pricked out, not necessarily each into its own pot, although I grow some this way to give away. Quite a number are grouped together in one bowl. I use plenty of drainage material, a good layer of charcoal pieces (which incidentally can be used time and time again) and Kerimure compost. Elsewhere I have cyclamen growing, also grouped in bowls. I grow those with the ornamental silver foliage because these are then decorative almost from the beginning and long before the flowers appear.

When someone tells me that he or she has never been successful in growing cyclamen, or perhaps African violets, another plant which is difficult, I recommend them to forget about buying mature plants and to begin instead with seeds. It is quite surprising how often one finds that the plants grow well. They become acclimatised to the environment from the very beginning, and very few plants turn out to be failures. Of course you might not grow them into such huge and splendid plants as those you would buy from one of the great nurseries, but you will get more satisfaction than disappointment from your venture. And you are almost certain to raise sufficient plants to have some available for passing on as gifts to your friends.

I find that little fibrous-rooted begonias are ideal for windowsill culture. These are the kinds usually grown for garden bedding. I grow them massed in bowls and have several about the house in bloom as I write. This way of displaying them is very attractive, several plants together, each with its own colour bloom, making a particularly bright and vivid decoration.

If you like hanging baskets try raising some of the *Begonia pendula* or basket type varieties. These will grow both indoors and out if you remember not to put them out until all danger of frost has past.

Blue flower enthusiasts would like browallia. These are easy to grow and very rewarding because they are so free flowering. The plants are much improved and kept neater if you remember to pinch out the growing tips from the stem ends occasionally. You can sow these at various times, in March for autumn flowers, during summer for winter and spring flowers. *Browallia speciosa* 'Major' is a fine species for winter flowering. There is also a white variety, 'Silver Stars'.

Some people become tremendous calceolaria enthusiasts. I have raised these plants on windowsills too, but they are not among my favourites, for I find that they need a little too much supporting and tending generally. However, they make splendid floral decorations in winter if you sow the seed in August. The only thing is that your home must be warm, because they cannot stand low night temperatures.

Cinerarias are beautifully flamboyant and easily raised from seed. However, they have one great drawback: they seem to attract every aphis in the locality. If you grow these pretty daisies you should use a systemic insecticide as soon as the plants are growing well, and keep on with it at regular intervals according to the instructions.

They are also demanding in the amounts of water they need when they are growing well. Unlike some plants, one should not wait on one's own convenience and allow the plant to flag a little until it is convenient to water it. Once a cineraria wilts it will never return to its first lovely freshness.

An easy, neat and fragrant plant is *Exacum affine*. When well grown it is absolutely smothered with little lavender-coloured starry flowers with bright golden centres. Sow the seed in spring for autumn and winter flowers.

We so often see just the bright pink variety of Busy Lizzie (*Impatiens sultanii*) growing in windows all over the country that there are many people who are surprised to learn that there are other hues. Try a packet of mixed seed and see just how pretty the variety can be. They look delightful mixed in a large but not deep container. If you have too many plants for indoors the surplus will grow anywhere in the garden, best in a shady place. Plant them out at the beginning of June.

You will need a comparatively high temperature to get them to germinate well, about 21° C., 70° F. The seeds usually take about three weeks to germinate. Keep the seed pans in full light: they do not require the usual period of darkness.

Primulas in variety will lighten the dark days of winter for you. If you like yellow, *Primula kewensis* 'Sungold', an improved type of the species, has fragrant flowers. *Primula obconica* is a great favourite of mine. I know of few pot plants which go on flowering for such a long time. One stem of flowers follows another so quickly that often the plant is a mass of blooms and these persist for weeks. Colours range from what I call primula pink through to deep violet blue. There is lavender, salmon, crimson and white. You can sow the seed in March for winter flowers, and in July for a spring show.

Poor man's orchid is the name given to the showy schizanthus, although some call it butterfly flower, but no matter what trivial name you give it the flowers continue to be as lovely as those of any pot plant. More than that, they are produced in great profusion. A well grown plant will be covered with flowers. At that time it really does resemble a great cloud of coloured butterflies. Think of scissors and you will remember the somewhat ungainly name, for it comes from schizo, to cut, and anthos a flower, which refers to the deeply cut corolla.

Those without central heating will be interested to learn that schizanthus does best under cool conditions and they need only enough heat in winter to protect the plants from frost. I like to grow these plants in deep vases, the kind I might use for very large flower arrangements. They look particularly good in pedestal types, copies of certain terrace pots, nicely classical in shape. I prick off five, seven or so plants into a large vase, and the result is a really lovely colour harmony.

You will find that it is essential to stake the plants, otherwise they will not only sprawl in a very untidy manner but they also will fail to bloom as well as when they grow upright.

You can stagger the flowering season remarkably well if you sow seed during August and September for winter, and from January to May for summer show.

Saintpaulias, or African violets, are splendid examples of a point I made earlier, that if you have had continued failure with flowering plants, try raising them from seed instead of buying fully grown plants. You will need a warm place in which to germinate the seed, somewhere with a temperature of about 21° C. or 70° F. The young seedlings must be shaded from the sun.

I grow many of these pretty plants and having tried them in all parts of the house I find that they grow best of all in a north-facing window, close to the glass in a warm and well-lit room.

Warmth is essential always. The temperature should never be allowed to fall below about 15° C., or 60° F., even at night. If it does, the plants tend to take on what I can only call a 'cold' appearance, and they will never flower well. A well-grown plant should keep flowering regulary. If by chance you fear a drop in the temperature during winter protect your pant by slipping it inside a large plastic bag until the temperature rises again. Incidentally, a high light intensity is important. If you are not sure if the place you have selected for your plants is light enough, hold your hand about four inches above the plant and see if a faint shadow is cast on the leaves. If it is, then there is sufficient light.

If all you have is a south window this is likely to be much too bright for saintpaulias, and you will be wise to protect your plants from the glare of the sun. This is important, because a hot sun really can burn the leaves and brown them badly. If the windows have net or curtains of some other fine material over them, the direct sun will do no harm. All the same, do be careful when you water the plants that no drops of water fall on the leaves, because this too could cause burning. The water drops combined with the sun shining through glass seem to make a burning glass.

It is said that saintpaulias need as much as 12 or 14 hours of good light before they will bloom really prolifically, so if your plants are not flowering as well as you think they should, you may be giving them too long a bed time. If you grow your plants on the windowsills of the living room, arrange to have them on the room side of the curtains during the long evenings, so that they get the benefit of your electric light.

These plants should always be plunged, for humidity is very important to them, and it is quite likely that they will need repotting each year. You can also divide large specimens in the spring. Take care never to plant them in too large pots or they will never thrive.

I once had a letter from a reader saying that she and her husband had recently returned from a holiday abroad, where for the first time they had seen the incredible *Strelitzia regina,* the Bird of Paradise flower. They had been so impressed with it that they wanted to grow some for themselves. Did I think that the plants could be raised from seed. I replied that they could, but explained also what a tricky business this could be. In the first place the plants take three or four years from seed before they will produce their flowers. Then there is the question of germination, where a soil temperature of about 20° C. is essential, in addition to a great deal of patience, for the seed will take six months or so to sprout. However, she wanted to try and I suggested that she sowed the seed in the usual way and put the container in a tightly sealed bag in the airing cupboard, inspecting it from time to time to make sure that the compost had not dried out. Years passed, and one day I received an ecstatic letter to say that the plants had actually flowered at last!

These are large plants, three to five feet tall, and I had a mental vision of two people in a little house being gradually pushed out by all those menacing potted birds of paradise!

I relate the story here merely as encouragement for any reader who might be wondering if windowsill cultivation is ever really worth while. It is.

15. Preventions and Cures

The beginner is usually far more worried about plants suffering from insect or disease attack than is necessary. There are very few insects and even fewer diseases which affect the well-grown house plant in the clean home, and those plants which seem almost inexplicably to sicken and die in the hands of some people have almost certainly died of some physiological disorder brought on by over-watering, over feeding, over-warming or some similar over-handling.

The overwhelming majority of the plants which we buy (as opposed to those raised by friends or grown ourselves) come from huge wholesale nurseries where hundreds of thousands of pounds are invested in greenhouses, equipment and stock to provide us with the hundreds of thousands of plants which we 'consume' each year. If some insect or disease attack were to sweep through those plants, together in such close proximity, enormous damage could be done and apalling losses suffered. For this reason the most careful eye is always kept on every plant, and a clinical cleanliness is maintained to avoid the possibility of any trouble. The best nurseries also maintain an inspection department, where teams of workers examine every plant leaving the premises to go to the major wholesale markets or retail establishments all over the country. So there is little possibility of any plant you bring into your home suffering from any pest or disease direct from the nursery.

However, we are all human, and occasions do arise when a plant may not receive the attention it requires before it comes into your hands. It is possible that it misses the inspection net at the nursery. It can possibly become infected with some insects in transit or in the large wholesale markets. The plant may be hanging about for some time before it is sold and consequently dry at the roots, or possibly in winter it may catch a chill through being stood in a draught or in an unheated shop.

So it is always wise when buying a plant to examine it with the greatest care before you make your purchase. The manager of even the most generous store will find it goes against the grain to refund the money for, or replace, a plant which may have been in your hands for some days before the incipient trouble becomes obviously apparent. Reject any plant with brown leaves and any whose leaves are limp and drooping. Make sure that the soil surface is moist. Do not accept any plant that is broken or is misshapen unless, like a Japanese bonsai tree, it has been carefully grown that way. Look carefully on the undersides of leaves and in what leaf and stem joints you can easily see for any evidences of insects, insect eggs or even past insect attack, and refuse the plant if any of these are visible. Distorted and discoloured leaves can mean that the plant once suffered from some insect attack and may still be suffering from a transmitted virus. Reject any plant which still carries the white or grey powdery residue on its leaves of an anti-pest or anti-disease spray. It may be good evidence of care by the grower, but why should you, the customer, have to clean your plant before it looks its best?

On the positive side look for a sturdy plant with good colour and all its foliage turgid and strong. It should be in a clean pot holding moist soil. If the plant has flowers these should be half open or less, rather than in full bloom, and there should be many buds still to open in the days to come. Both plant and soil should have a sweet and wholesome smell.

Having selected and bought your plant, make sure that it is properly wrapped before you take it home. Even in the fine days of spring and summer draughts and drying winds can cause damage to a sensitive plant, which, after all, has until now spent most of its life in the artificial protection of the greenhouse. The pot should be wrapped, of course, to save you soiling gloves, hands or clothes, but equally important is the plant itself. In winter make quite sure that the entire plant is enveloped in some kind of wrapping paper. Today many plants come prepacked, sometimes even prebagged, and the protective covering they receive in this manner is probably sufficient.

When you get your plant home you are on your own. Some plant growers affix little labels to their products naming the plant and giving brief instructions for its care. Retail florists or garden shops sometimes fix their own labels, or those produced by one of the trade or professional organisations. These labels and these instructions are always helpful, and the advice they give cannot be beaten. Keep the label, not necessarily on the plant but conveniently, and refer to it when necessary so that you always know what you are doing.

However, these instructions frequently omit one vital piece of advice. This is that when you first get your plant home, regardless of what type it is, sun lover like cactus or bog plant like cyperus, make sure that the soil is thoroughly and uniformly wet. The best way to do this is to immerse the entire pot in a bucket of water. Leave it there until bubbles cease to rise from the surface, then remove it and allow it to drain thoroughly. This drainage period is just as important as the watering, for as the water rushes through the drainage hole at the base of the pot it drags after it fresh air into the soil spaces vacated. Thus the roots have both water and air, two essentials for their health.

If it is convenient for you, this total immersion method of watering is good for most plants three or four times a year during the warmest months. It is more efficient than using a watering can, a kettle or the teapot, which sometimes results in one section of the soil in the pot receiving no water at all for several successive waterings. If this happens this soil becomes brick hard and will be difficult to water at all other than by immersion.

However, the total immersion system is so thorough that the drainage and drying out period must be equally efficient. Allow the plant to drain properly before it is placed in its decorative position in the home, and then allow it to become almost dry before you water it again, whichever method you use. The roots should be almost dry.

Now, having brought your plant home and watered it thoroughly, where will you decide to put it? The answer to this is that you put it wherever you think it will look best. The plant is there to please you, to add to the general decoration of your home. If the position you choose is not suitable for the plant then it will soon show you by drooping, by yellowing or dropping its leaves, and you must then decide whether to find another and more suitable position for the plant or whether to throw it out and buy another.

I believe very firmly that plants are in our homes to please us and that we must not become slaves to them. Nevertheless, there are certain guidelines to plant positions in the home that can help us all, both by increasing the general decorative effect and by extending the healthy lives of our plants.

The first thing to understand about growing plants in the home is that the most important factor for success is good light. Light is more important than warmth, and on a par with water as an essential. Earlier in this book I said that as a general rule the thicker and darker green the leaf the less light the plant will need. The opposite is also true. The finer and more delicate the leaf and the more colour it contains, then the more light it will need. Flowering plants, the most colourful of all house plants, must have good light to flourish. But good light does not mean sunlight. Only cacti and some other succulents require full sun for their health, and most other house plants find it too much for them.

So if good light is such a vital ingredient to plant health it should be taken seriously. Fortunately most homes today are well windowed and plenty of light is allowed inside. The windowsill is usually a good place for most plants, but where a room is light and airy they can so frequently look at their best on the other side of the room from the windows, for here they get god light and yet turn their growing leaves into rather than out of the room.

Beware if the windows are ill-fitting and allow draughts to whistle through onto your plants, for this they all hate and will show their unhappiness by drooping and shedding leaves. Again, if the windows are curtained off at nights against the cold and dark, try to make sure that the plants are kept on the warm side of the curtains rather than against glass, which may even become frosted during the night. Hot air is as damaging as cold, so keep plants out of the direct effects of all types of heating.

The plunge pot method of keeping house plants which I have so frequently advocated in earlier pages is an excellent means of maintaining steady day and night temperatures for your plants, for the extra pot and the insulating properties of the peat or other material protects that plant pot and the tender roots it contains from any changes of temperature that may occur. But, as I have said earlier, very few house plants require high temperatures for their well-being. For most it is quite sufficient if they are kept just a few degrees above outside temperatures. Most plants are better in winter time in the cooler parts of the house rather than in the general living room, which sometimes gets both very warm and very stuffy. Plants prefer the cooler and cleaner air of halls or bedrooms, and if the light in these is poor, remember that the ordinary domestic incandescent lamp is a fairly efficient provider of light in the wavelengths necessary for plants. Any plant kept in a fairly dark hallway, for example, will improve with a few hours of good light from an ordinary bulb. For optimum efficiency this should be centred up to two feet above the plant, no nearer in case the warmth harms plant tissue.

These points about the positioning of plants in the home are made with an eye to maintaining the plants in good health for as long as possible. A plant in good health is not only more attractive than one that is either ill or sulking, it is less likely to suffer from or give in to insect or disease attack. A healthy plant is a strong plant.

Every plant coming from a good nursery will be growing in a soil or a compost which already contains sufficient food to nourish the plant for between two and six months. So any new plant you bring home will not require feeding for, shall we say, three months, and after this should be fed only weak and dilute liquid food solutions for some time, depending on the time of year.

Just as more plants are killed by over-watering than any other ill treatment, so many plants are over-fed and live a short, bilious, unhappy and unprepossessing life. A cat or a dog, for example, will reject food if too much is placed befort it. But a plant must accept whatever is fed into its soil, and this is generally far too much.

There is little to choose between the various proprietary plant foods. All contain much the same ingredients in much the same proportions, and generally speaking their recommendations for use are sound. But we ourselves must make up our minds how we wish to grow our plants. If we follow the recommendations of the plant food manufacturers we will probably achieve optimum growth for our plants. They will put out young, fresh and attractive foliage, will open large and colourful blooms, will reach upwards to the ceiling – and quickly outgrow the corner in which they have been placed!

My own opinion is that plants should be fed only sufficiently to maintain them in good health (and consequently good appearance) for long periods and allow them to grow very slowly. After all, if we accept that plants are here to decorate our homes this must mean that they are more or less in proportion with their surroundings when they are first introduced. If they grow large and unwieldy they will lose their decorative value, but they will do this gradually and we will be unlikely to notice until it is too late to do anything about it. But if we feed our plants very lightly they will remain in proportion with their environment for much longer periods.

All plants must rest at some time of the year, and most (but not all) choose the colder and darker days of winter for this resting period. During this time every pressure on them is to grow, because they are receiving artificial stimuli from the unnatural warmth and the unnatural light. So we should cut out feeding entirely for the winter months and allow the plants to rest and recover for the season to come.

In the spring, as soon as evidence of new growth is noticed, feeding should start. It is best to start gently, lead up to maximum rates, and then to taper off as gently as you began. In other words, in early spring begin feeding your plants with a liquid solution perhaps one quarter the recommended strength. Gradually increase this until in high summer full-strength feeds are given for a brief period and then decrease the strength gradually until no food at all is given during the winter. Remember, also, that to a plant the summer depends on day length rather than temperature. This is why plants sometimes appear to be putting out their spring growth surprisingly early. They are merely responding to the increased length of day and the shorter night, irrespective of the cold outside the window.

We have discussed light, watering and feeding, but have so far said nothing about the lack of humidity, which is always difficult to overcome. All plants need a certain amount of humidity and most need more than we can given them in the average home, particularly today with the dry warmth of central heating making the place so comfortable for humans and so dry and arid for plants. If we plunge our plants inside other, larger containers and keep the space between the two filled with some constantly moist medium such as peat, we will be doing something for these plants, for the moisture will constantly be evaporating into the air and providing a tiny microclimate of humidity around the foliage of the plants. So this is certainly something worth doing, and under certain circumstances it may be the only thing we can do.

On the other hand, even for our own sakes it is sometimes advisable to soften and moisten the arid air which we breathe, and thus improve conditions for our furnishings and indeed for our complexions. There are various types of humidifiers on the market, some simple water tanks to be attached to radiators, and others more complex electrical appliances which spread microscopic droplets of water through the atmosphere. All are helpful to some degree, for we do not aim to achieve bathroom humidity throughout the house, only to take away just a little of the aridity. This can, in fact, be achieved merely by placing about the house in the more heated rooms little areas of water. These can take the form of a hidden bowl, or a pan filled with bright seashells or attractive stones, or even a large flower bowl with just a few flowers in it and plenty of water. And little indoor miniature fountains not only look attractive, but also humidify the air.

For plants which require a greater degree of humidity than can be provided by these means an occasional spray may be the answer. Little sprayers or atomisers can be bought quite cheaply, and it is possible in many places about the home to use one of these on a plant without causing any harm to the surrounding furnishings. It is not necessary to soak the plant, only to moisten the leaves very lightly. Most small plants, of course, can be removed easily enough to the bathroom or to the garden for this treatment, and in fact the best means of spraying most conveniently sized house plants is to put them out of doors during a mild spring shower.

It is not easy to tell how dry is the atmosphere in the home, for unlike the thermometer built in to us all we have no hygrometer. However, one can be bought quite cheaply and is worth having if you take your house plants seriously. Some even have, marked on the dial, the recommended relative humidity advised for certain types of plants. I try to keep sections of my home at a figure of between 55 and 65, yet I sometimes find that during the cold days of winter this figure will sometimes drop to about 40 before I notice it, which just shows how insensitive we are to this particular facet of the atmosphere. Opening a window for a few minutes will mean only a tiny drop in temperature but will enormously increase the relative humidity. Another means to obtain an early and speedy increase in humidity is to boil a kettle for a few minutes, and allow the steam to fill the room.

Certain plants, such as saintpaulias, benefit greatly by an occasional humidity bath, and one way of providing this without much trouble is as follows. Take the plant, and if it is not already in a cover or plunge pot, place it inside another container which has no drainage holes and is only slightly larger. Then place this inside another considerably larger bowl or basin into which should be poured boiling water. The steam from this rises up and surrounds the little plant sitting on an island in the centre. Leave the plant there until the water has cooled. The humidity bath will have done it the world of good.

All these hints for the successful cultivation of your plants are put forward as a preface, so to speak, to a short section on house plant pests and house plant diseases. I have said before and I cannot stress too strongly that healthy plants shrug off sickness.

Much sickness originates in insect attack, so let us first look at what pests we might possibly find on our house plants. The most likely is the familiar aphid, the greenfly which is attracted to so many of our garden plants, particularly roses, and is so easily imported into the house on a bunch brought inside for decoration or which, indeed, can fly eagerly through the open windows of summer onto a succulent feast of tender young house plant growth.

Greenfly are suckers. They pierce a leaf or tender shoot, and suck at the sap. If they have come from another plant which has been infected with some other sickness there is every possibility that they will infect the house plant with this same virus, or whatever. Greenfly are also prodigious breeders. Females produce large numbers of living young which almost immediately set to breeding themselves, and in no time whole colonies exist.

Greenfly can be seen on the young shoots of plants and early action taken to clear them. If, however, your plants do not get daily inspection or attention, the distortion and discoloration of the leaves may indicate that something is wrong.

There are special insecticides which are aimed specifically against aphids and there are others which are designed more generally for garden pests as a whole. Some kill by contact, and some kill by poisoning the sap of the plant, so that when the aphid sucks it is drinking poison. The second type is known as a systemic insecticide, as it works through the system of the plant. Systemics can be watered into the soil so that they are taken up by the roots and spread through the plant. The only trouble here is that this may take a day or two, where our aim is to get rid of the insects immediately.

Before any insecticide is used it must be understood very clearly that these are poisons. Almost all will say on their labels that they should be used only as garden insecticides. This I must emphasise. No insecticide shoud ever be sprayed in the home, except, of course, some of the proprietary fly killers designed specifically to be used indoors. These, incidentally, will be successful, if used as a superficial first killer on green-fly.

But generally, all plants which are to be sprayed with an insecticide must be taken outside into the open air before they are treated, and they should be allowed to dry out again before they are brought indoors. Once the attack has been dealt with and the insects have disappeared, it is wise to add a small dose of systemic insecticide to the water once a month or so, as this will almost certainly 'nip in the bud' any insect build-up in the future summer months.

For some small plants the total immersion system can be used as a means of clearing aphis attack. In this case use what are called white oils, and make a solution at the required strength. The entire plant, pot and all, can then be submerged in this solution to clear attack from the entire plant. Where the plant is too large to be submerged like this it is possible to sponge or paint it with the white-oil solution, seeing that the liquid pene-trates every little crack and cranny in the joints. These white oils leave the foliage with a pleasant, clean and healthy sheen. They are used extensively by nurserymen for a final cleaning of their plants before they are shipped off to market.

Attacks from greenfly cannot really be prevented, but attacks from another insidious little pest which goes under the erroneous name of red spider should never happen, for they take place only when the atmosphere is dry – too dry – and in winter or summer. The red spider is a mite, not a spider at all, and it is not red, it is a rusty brown. It is almost impossible to see as it is so small, and if seen at all with the naked eye it will be only a tiny dot.

Suspect red spider if some leaves begin to discolour, to go brown and become brittle and drop off. There is a difference in the appearance of the leaves when the plant is merely dry, for with red spider they seem to have a more unhealthy appearance. The mites usually collect on the underside of the leaves, and one means of detecting them is to feel this leaf between finger and thumb. If it is vaguely rough, then the pests are probably present. They make something like a web and this can sometimes be seen with the naked eye, but a better way of recognising this is to blow a little powder or the ash of a cigarette onto the back of a leaf which you consider may be infested. The web-like material will hold this powder or ash in its strands, and if the material merely falls off when blown onto the back of the leaf then the trouble is not red spider.

Some of the proprietary insecticides will clear red spider, but they need to be applied under some pressure and the whole of the plant will need wetting thoroughly, so the plant will have to be taken outside for this. Again, if the plant is small it will be possible to dip it complete in a bucket of white oils and this will do the trick.

To ward off future attacks of red spider always make sure that your plants live in a mildly humid atmosphere, and if you find that any one plant is subject to attack, give it an occasional spray with clean rain water.

Mealy bug is yet another pest which occasionally appears on some house plants. As its name suggests, it is revealed as a white or greyish mealy or fluffy spot, almost like a tiny tuft of cotton wool. Inside the fluff or the meal is a little bug-like creature busily sucking the sap out of the plant. The longer the mealy bug goes undetected the more little bugs there will be under the covering of fluff. On a large vine you may suddenly see one of these little tufts, and on examining the plant more closely discover dozens more, perhaps even hundreds. As a rule they are discovered before they go too far and can be picked off individually.

A spray of insecticide will clear them, but this must be applied with great strength to penetrate the waxy fluff in which they hide. So an infested plant will certainly have to be taken outside for treatment. Alternatively you can go over the plant very carefully with a matchstick dipped in white oils and scrape away at each little white tuft until the reddish brown insect is seen and killed. This requires some patience, but on the other hand it is easier on many occasions than a complete spraying programme.

As this is another sucking insect it is possible to prevent a real infestation by watering the most susceptible plants once a month or so with a systemic insecticide. This will ensure that if mealy bug once starts it will quickly be killed and no new major attack will build up.

The last of the very few insects that I propose to discuss is another little sucking insect known as scale. It appears to be something like a very small louse-like insect or a small wood louse, which attaches itself to the underside of the leaf, forms a hard, shell-like covering which serves as protection both for itself and for its eggs and young. This shell also protects it from most sprays, but as the pest is another sucker it can be killed by using a systemic insecticide.

Fortunately a heavy infestation is comparatively rare on any plants that receive regular care and attention, so it will normally be a case of identifying the pest and removing it by hand. It clings very tightly to the surface of the leaf, and will have to be scraped off with a knife, with a matchstick or even (most efficient this!) with a finger or thumb nail.

There is really no excuse for these or any other insects to appear on your plants, for their appearance suggests very strongly that you are not examining or caring for your plants as you should. Nevertheless, pests do appear, some as strange as slugs, earthworms – ants even – which seem to me to indicate a degree of carelessness entirely incompatible with the keeping of house plants at all!

The diseases that attack house plants are even fewer in number than the pests, and are nearly always caused by bad cultivation or poor and unsatisfactory conditions. Various mildews, root rots, wilts, moulds and fungus attacks are sometimes, though very rarely, seen. They can usually be cured if caught in time by correcting the fault in culture that caused the disease in the first place.

Mildews are usually caused by over-watering. They appear as a white powder on leaf surfaces. They can also be caused on some plants by over-crowding and by insufficient ventilation. Several of the proprietary fungicides can be used to control mildew, but always make quite sure that the fungicide and the plant are compatible, and that it is applied exactly in accordance with the maker's instructions.

Wilts and root rots are again nearly always caused by over-watering, and too often the disease has progressed too far before it is diagnosed. One reason for this is that an over-watered plant frequently presents the same symptoms as one which is dry at the roots, so more water is given in an attempt to rescue the plant, and this merely hastens its end.

If it is discovered that root rot or wilt has set in because the plant has been standing in a puddle or a bog, then it is possible to leave the plant to dry out by itself, withholding all water for some weeks. If a more speedy action is thought necessary, it is possible to knock the plant from its pot, gently scrape away some of the wet and soggy soil from the roots, and replace this with fresh, dry soil or compost, repotting again in the same container.

Moulds on house plants usually grow on the sooty or sticky excreta of aphids, so the best way to prevent them is to avoid the aphids themselves. If they do appear, grey or black and powdery, then a good fungicide will usually clear them.

Very occasionally a house plant will be attacked by a virus of some kind, probably brought by aphids, and the plant will twist, curl, contort itself and give every evidence of the agony through which it is passing. Nothing can be done for a plant like this, and the best thing to do is to burn it, complete with pot and soil, as soon as possible, so as to lessen any possible chance that other plants might be infected.

In fact, although I have mentioned here brief rescue operations if plants are attacked by insects or diseases, I would be the first to say that if a plant is badly attacked by anything then the best thing to do is to get rid of it as soon as you can, and replace it with a healthy plant. Most of us are far too senti-mental about our plants and hang on to them long after they should have been thrown out.

The only excuse for growing house plants is to decorate the home. If plants are not at their best they are no longer decora-tive, and if they are not at their best there is always the danger that they will infect some neighbouring plant.

We have learnt, however, that the best way to ensure that a plant is strong and healthy and disease-free is to grow it well, something well within the capabilities of us all. If this little book helps only one person to do this then I will consider the writing well worth while.

Index

Acidanthera, 106
Adromischus, 93
Aechmea, 24
Aechmea propagation, 28
Aeonium, 92
Aeration, 17
Aerial roots, 69
African violets, 20, 114, 115, 117
Air-layering, 37, 73
Aloe, 46, 84
Amaryllis, 103, 106
Ananas, 27
Anomatheca, 107
Anthurium, 68, 111
Aphids, 21, 116, 128
Araceae, 68
Aroid, 68
Arums, 68
Asparagus fern, 44
Aspect and positions, 123
Aspidistra, 42
Astrophytum, 86
Azalea, 16, 110, 111

Barrel cacti, 86
Begonia, 112, 115
Beloperone, 112
Billbergia, 28
Bletia or Bletilla, 104
Blood lilies, 105
Botanical terms, 32
Bottle gardens, 50
Bowl gardens, 94
Bromeliads, 25
Browallia, 115
Bryophyllum, 97
Bulb fibre, 100
Bulb fibre, to make, 102
Bulbs in pebbles and water, 100
Bulbs in water, 99
Bulb ripening, 106
Busy Lizzie, 116
Butia, 51

Cacti, 16, 19, 83
Cacti from seed, 89
Cacti identification, 83-84
Cacti soil or compost, 88
Cacti spines, to remove, 88
Calla lilies, 68
Calceolaria, 116
Cereae, 86
Cereus cacti, 86
Cephalocereus, 86
Chamaecereus, 86
Chamaerops, 48
Chamaedora, 49
Chinese fan palm, 51
Chlorophytum, 39-42, 66
Christmas, bulbs to flower for, 101-102
Christmas cactus, 87
Cissus, 74
Cinerarias, 116
Cocos, 48-49
Coleus, 63
Coleus cuttings, 64
Commelina, 82
Commelinaceae, 78
Containers for bulbs, 102
Convallaria, 107
Cotyledons, 93, 97
Crab cactus, 91
Crassula, 95
Crassulaceae, 92
Cryptanthus, 27
Cyclamen, 112, 115
Curly palm, 51
Cuttings, 61, 79

Date palm, 50
Date stones, to germinate, 50-51
Derris dust, 47
Dicotyledons, 42
Diseases, 120
Draughts, 59, 123
Dwarf date palm, 51

Easter cactus, 91
Echeveria, 92, 94, 96
Environment, 12
Epiphyllum, 87, 90
Epiphyte, 25, 69, 86
Erica, 113
Eucomis, 105
Euphorbia pulcherrima, 113
Exacum, 116

Fatshedera, 60
Fatsia, 58
Feeding plants, 125
Ficus, 31
Ficus, to water, 36–37
Flowers of the desert, 85
Flowering plants from seed, 114–115
Fungicides, 131
Garland cacti, 85
Glazed containers, 76
Glecoma, 63
Gloxinia, 113
Grafting cacti, 85, 88
Greenfly, 128
Ground ivy, 63

Haemanthus, 106
Hanging baskets, 41, 81
Heather, 16, 113
Hedera, 54
Hedgehog cactus, 86
Hippeastrum, 103, 106
Howea, 51
Humidity, 20, 126
Hyacinth, 99, 101
Hyacinths in glasses, 99

Impatiens, 116
Insecticides, 21
Insect pests, 120
Ivy leaves, falling, 57
Ivy, propagation, 58, 66, 72

Jade plant, 95
Jacobean lily, 106
John Innes Composts, 14

Kalanchoe, 95
Kalosanthes, 95
Kangaroo vine, 74
Kentia, 51

Labiates, 62
Lapeirousia, 107
Layering plants, 42, 75
Leaf-flowering cactus, 87
Leaves, dropping, 37, 129
Leaves, to clean, 34–36
Leaves, turning yellow, 23
Light, 123
Light intensity, 56, 79
Liliaceae, 42
Lilies, 104
Lily-of-the-valley, 107
Livingstona, 51
Living stones, 93

Mammilaria, 85
Mealy bug, 23, 130
Mesembryanthemum, 84
Mildew, 131
Miniature gardens, 88
Miniature grape-ivy, 77
Monocotyledons, 42
Monstera, 68, 71, 72
Mother-in-law's tongue, 45
Mould, 132

Narcissi, 102
Narcissi in pebbles, 100
Neanthe bella, 49
Neoregelia, 29
Nepeta, 63
Nerines, 107
Nidularium, 29
Night-blooming cacti, 86
Nomenclature, 40
Nopalxochia, 91

Offsets, 28
Old man cactus, 86
Oliveranthus, 96
Opuntia, 85
Orchid cacti, 91

Palms, 48
Palms, from seed, 51
Palms, re-potting, 51–52
Partridge plant, 46
Peanut cactus, 86
Pereskieae, 85
Philodendron, 66, 68
Phoenix, 50, 51
Pineapple, 27
Pineapple propagation, 29
Pineapple flower, 105
Plant foods, 13, 15
Plant pests, 21
Plant rosettes, 93
Plant sickness, 120–133
Plectranthus, 61
Plunging plants, 20, 26, 49, 124
Poinsettias, 110, 113
Poor man's orchid, 117
Pot drainage, 52
Pot sizes, 19
Potting soils and composts, 13–18
Prickly pear, 85, 86
Primulas, 116
Puddle pots, 65, 76, 79

Rain water, 35
Red spider, 22, 129
Repotting, 13
Resting plants, 125
Rhoea, 82
Rhoicissus, 15, 66, 75
Rio tradescantia, 79
Rochea, 95
Room pines, 27
Roman hyacinths, 101
Roots, 12
Root rot, 132
Rosularias, 94
Rubber plant, 31

Saintpaulias, 114, 117
Sansevieria, 45, 84
Saxifraga sarmentosa, 41
Scale insect, 23, 131
Schizanthus, 117
Schlumbergera, 91

Sedum, 94, 97
Seed sowing, 63
Setcreasea, 82
Smilax, 44
Soils, 13
Soilless and no-soil composts, 14, 100
Soluble foods, 15, 76
Spathiphyllum, 68
Spider plant, 40
Spiderwort, 78
Sports, 54
Sprekelia, 106
Star cactus, 86
Stolons, 40
Strelitzia, 119
Streptocarpus, 114
Succulent, definition, 83
Succulents, 17
Swiss Cheese plant, 68
Syngonium, 73
Systemic insecticides, 22, 128

Temperatures, 124
Thanksgiving cactus, 91
Thatch leaf palm, 51
Tillandsia, 30
Top dressing, 52
Tradescantia, 66, 78
Tulips, 102

Umbilicus, 94

Vitaceae, 74
Vriesia, 30

Wandering Jew, 78
Wandering sailor, 78
Wardian cases, 23
Watering, 16–20, 36–37, 122
White oils, 129, 130
Wilt, 132
Woolly rose, 97

Zantedeschias, 68
Zebrina, 80
Zygocactus, 91